DEDICATION

For the people and places of the Lowcountry.
And to the memory of Pat Conroy, who
introduced us to his beloved home.

"We are here because of our love of this incomparable portion of the earth. We are here because we have Lowcountry hearts."
–Pat Conroy, *A Lowcountry Heart*

Lowcountry boil on the water
at Hudson's Seafood House on the Docks
Courtesy of Hilton Head Island-Bluffton VCB

100 THINGS TO DO IN THE SOUTH CAROLINA LOWCOUNTRY BEFORE YOU DIE

Hilton Head Island
Courtesy of Hilton Head Island-Bluffton VCB

100 THINGS TO DO IN THE SOUTH CAROLINA LOWCOUNTRY BEFORE YOU DIE

LYNN AND CELE SELDON

Reedy Press
PO Box 5131
St. Louis, MO 63139, USA
reedypress.com

Library of Congress Control Number: 2025936734

ISBN: 9781681065960

Cover photo in public domain

Design by Jill Halpin

Printed in Canada
25 26 27 28 29   5 4 3 2 1

CONTENTS

Acknowledgments xiii

Preface xv

Food and Drink

1. Taste the Lowcountry at Lowcountry Produce 2
2. Say Bonjour to Hilton Head Social Bakery 4
3. Get Your Veggie On at Herban Market & Cafe 5
4. Quench Your Thirst at Burnt Church Distillery 6
5. Feed Your Hunger at Roxbury Mercantile 8
6. Dine in a Mansion at Ribaut Social Club 9
7. Eat Everything but the Oink at Rizer's Pork & Produce 10
8. Obey the Urge to Dine at SERG Restaurants 12
9. Taste the Sea at Locals Raw Bar 13
10. Dive Deeply into Southern Cooking at Bucky's Seafood 14
11. Head to the Countryside for Country Cookin' at Harold's Country Club 16
12. Savor a Beaufort Trifecta at Plums, Saltus, and Hearth 17
13. Learn to Cook at the Culinary Institute of the South 18
14. Coast on Over to Benny's Coastal Kitchen 20
15. Support Local Farmers at Lowcountry Farmers Markets 22

16. Say Cheers to Shellring Aleworks 24
17. Get Fishy at ACE Basin Fish Camp 25
18. Eat Farm-to-Fork at FARM 26
19. Head to Hudson's Seafood House on the Docks 27
20. Feast on Finger-Lickin' Fried Chicken 28
21. Enjoy Breakfast, Brunch, or Lunch at Magnolia Cafe 30
22. See the Ugly Fish at Whaley's 32
23. Drink and Eat Well at Blacksheep X Sabbatical 33
24. Take a Taste of Cottage Life 34
25. Eat Tasty Coastal 'Cue in the Lowcountry 36

Music and Entertainment

26. Enjoy Daily Live Music Year-Round at Tiki Hut 40
27. Support All the Arts at the Center for the Arts 42
28. Celebrate Hollywood in Hampton at the Palmetto Theater 43
29. Splash into the Beaufort Water Festival 44
30. Listen Up at the Jazz Corner 45
31. See a Show at the Arts Center of Coastal Carolina 46
32. Take In a Performance at Colleton Civic Center and Hampton St. Auditorium 47
33. Go to the Movies with Beaufort Tours 48
34. Enjoy Dinner and a Movie at Park Plaza Cinema 50
35. Get Your Groove On with Street Music on Paris Avenue 51

36. Be Entertained at Lowcountry Celebration Park 52

37. Listen to Live Music on the Water at Pressley's at the Marina 53

38. Rub Elbows with the Stars at the Beaufort International Film Festival 54

39. Make Music at the Kazoobie Kazoo Museum & Factory 56

40. Get Your Fill of Live Music, Grub, and Views at The Fillin' Station 57

Sports and Recreation

41. Spend the Day at the Beach at Hunting Island State Park 60

42. Get Outside with Coastal Expeditions 62

43. Watch Golf Greats at the RBC Heritage Golf Tournament 63

44. Sleep at the Beach at Edisto Beach State Park 64

45. Get on Two Wheels with Wheelz Hilton Head 65

46. Nurture Nature at Pinckney Island National Wildlife Refuge ... 66

47. Enjoy Disc Golf and the Water at Sergeant Jasper Park 67

48. Explore a Lowcountry Paradise at Montage Palmetto Bluff 68

49. Get Adventurous with Outside Hilton Head 69

50. Go Wild in Walterboro 70

51. Slither Over to Edisto Island Serpentarium 71

52. Get Healthier at Hilton Head Health Wellness Resort & Spa ... 72

53. Stay in a CCC-Built Cabin on the Edisto River 73

54. Get on the Water with Edisto Watersports & Tackle 74

55. Take a Trip to Famed Fripp Island 75

56. Explore Lowcountry Wild Wonders at Donnelley Wildlife Management Area 76
57. Get Out on the Spanish Moss Trail 77
58. Plan a Hilton Head Island Getaway to The Sea Pines Resort 78
59. Experience Primitive Lowcountry Coastline Life at Botany Bay... 80
60. Beach It on Hilton Head Island 82

Culture and History

61. Get the Lowdown on the Lowcountry at a Visitors Center 86
62. Get to Know the Prince of Scribes at the Pat Conroy Literary Center 88
63. Plunge into Lowcountry Marine Heritage 89
64. Celebrate Gullah Culture at Historic Penn Center 90
65. Uncover the Wonders of the Lowcountry at the Coastal Discovery Museum 92
66. Explore Lowcountry Culture at the Colleton Museum & Farmers Market 93
67. Honor America's History at the Reconstruction Era National Historical Park 94
68. Get a Fill-Up of Local History at the Morris Center for Lowcountry Heritage 96
69. Praise the Past at Old Sheldon Church Ruins 98
70. See the Making of Marines at Parris Island 99
71. Learn about the Lowcountry's Rich Gullah Culture 100
72. Admire Antebellum Architecture at the John Mark Verdier House 101

73. Explore America's First Self-Governed Town of Freedmen...... 102

74. Get Carried Away by a Carriage Tour in Historic Beaufort..... 103

75. Appreciate Authentic Lowcountry Art and History at LyBensons' Gallery 104

76. Glimpse into the Past in Colleton County 105

77. Relive Local History at the Beaufort History Museum 106

78. Hop a Boat to Quiet Daufuskie Island 107

79. Kid Around at the Sandbox Children's Museum 108

80. Explore Local History at The Edisto Island Museum 109

Shopping and Fashion

81. Book It to a Lowcountry Bookstore 112

82. Get Your Art On at the South Carolina Artisans Center 114

83. Feed Your Kitchen Hunger at Cook on Bay 115

84. Find the Perfect Piece in a Lowcountry Antiques Store 116

85. Channel Your Inner Artist at SOBA Gallery 118

86. Gather, Shop, and Be You at Birdie James 119

87. Bring a Touch of Southeast Asia into Your Home 120

88. Do a Little Retail Therapy at Eggs'n'tricities 121

89. Take Home a Taste of the Lowcountry 122

90. Reflect on Art at Beaufort River Glass 123

91. Become One with the Barefoot Contessa at Cassandra's Kitchen 124

92. Carry the Island Spirit with Spartina 449 125

93. Shop with Sass at Sassafras on Carteret 126
94. Bask in Bivalve Bric-a-Brac at Bluffton General Store 127
95. Fill Your Glass at ta·ca·rón 128
96. Celebrate American Crafts at With These Hands Gallery 129
97. Get Everything for the Home at Grayco Hardware & Home 130
98. Make Your Way to Macdonald MarketPlace 131
99. Roll on Over to Rollers Wine & Spirits 132
100. Go Big on the Pig 133

Activities by Season 134
Suggested Itineraries 136
Index 139

ACKNOWLEDGMENTS

As transplants to the Lowcountry, we have fallen in love with the people who have so graciously welcomed us to this unique part of the world. First and foremost, we want to thank the Lowcountry's world-class travel and tourism organizations and the leaders there who were a huge help: Peach Morrison with Lowcountry and Resort Islands Tourism Commission; Robb Wells with Visit Beaufort, Port Royal & Sea Islands; and Charlie Clark with the Hilton Head Island-Bluffton Chamber of Commerce. Thanks also to all the places, attractions, businesses, and restaurants that we reached out to for inclusion in this book—your assistance was invaluable. And to our friends who offered suggestions on what to include in the book and supported our efforts from the very beginning, this love letter to the Lowcountry is for all of you.

Carriage tour in historic Beaufort
Courtesy of Visit Beaufort

PREFACE

Researching and writing this tribute to the Lowcountry has greatly renewed our appreciation of where we live. The Lowcountry is consistently ranked as one of the world's top destinations, and this book provides a wide range of wonderful possibilities to pursue, whether you are a first-time visitor or a long-time resident.

For the purposes of this book, we are considering the "Lowcountry" to include the people, places, history, culture, food, vegetation, wildlife, and climate of the South Carolina coast from Edisto Island to Daufuskie Island. Although Charleston and Savannah are part of the Lowcountry geographically, we have covered these treasures previously in our books *100 Things to Do in Charleston Before You Die* and *100 Things to Do in Savannah Before You Die.*

With so many unique things to see and do, we had a difficult time narrowing down our list of "100 Things" for the Lowcountry. We'd love to hear about your experiences with our choices and learn about other possibilities. Find us on Facebook and Instagram at @SeldonInk and tag your own #100ThingsLowcountry.

—Lynn and Cele Seldon

Lowcountry shrimp and oysters
Courtesy of Hilton Head Island-Bluffton VCB

FOOD AND DRINK

1

TASTE THE LOWCOUNTRY
AT LOWCOUNTRY PRODUCE

This charming hotspot with three Lowcountry locations offers so much to those who want a taste of the Lowcountry. It's a go-to destination for freshly baked Lowcountry favorites, like tomato pie and buttermilk cheddar biscuits. It's also a restaurant serving breakfast, brunch, and lunch classics, including avocado toast; brioche French toast; green tomato pickle stack; Big Fat French Salad (warm red-skinned potatoes, bacon, goat cheese, and tomatoes over romaine dressed with a lemon Dijon vinaigrette); po boys; and the ever-popular Ooey Gooey, with melted pimento cheese, applewood bacon, and garlic pepper jelly. Plus, it's a take-away café, with comfort food specialties like pimento cheese, chicken salad, and pot pie; a cannery featuring house-made sauces, pickles, dips, jams, chutneys, and chow chows; a sundries shop selling grits, teas, and granola; and even a kitchen and home decor shop to take home a piece of the Lowcountry.

1919 Trask Pkwy., Lobeco, 843-846-9438
302 Carteret St., Beaufort, 843-322-1900
71 Lighthouse Rd., Hilton Head Island, 843-686-3003
lowcountryproduce.com

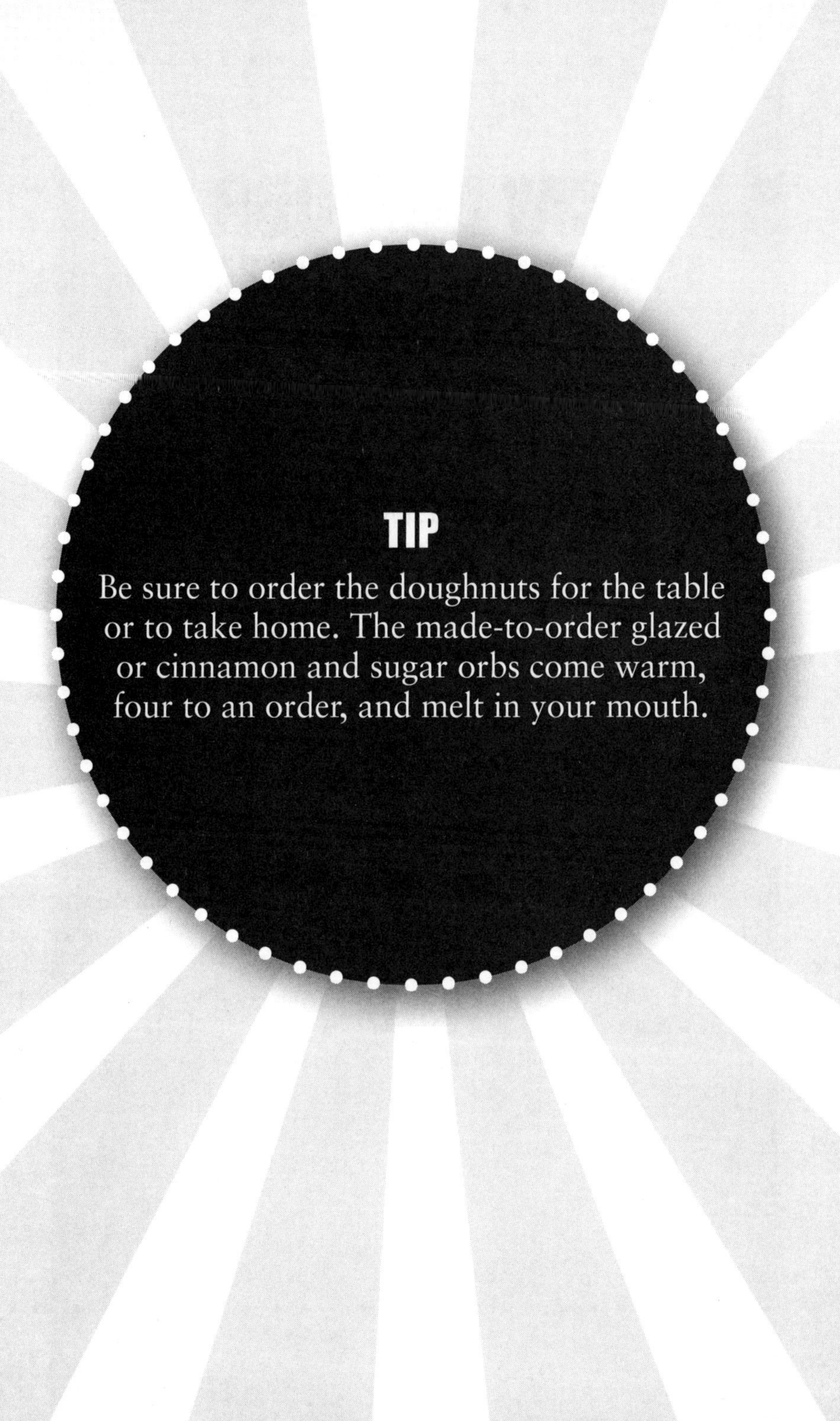

TIP

Be sure to order the doughnuts for the table or to take home. The made-to-order glazed or cinnamon and sugar orbs come warm, four to an order, and melt in your mouth.

SAY BONJOUR
TO HILTON HEAD SOCIAL BAKERY

Appealing to more than Francophiles, a stop in Hilton Head Social Bakery is like walking into an authentic French bakery and pâtisserie. Owned and operated by award-winning French chef, pastry chef, and master baker Philippe Feret—who started apprenticing in his father's Paris bakery from the age of 5—the display cases are brimming with legitimate French pastries, croissants, more than a dozen flavors of fresh fruit tarts, eclairs, macarons, napoleons, and so much more. Stop for breakfast and indulge in sweet or savory confections and a full complement of organic fair trade coffee drinks and a teeming selection of teas. Or, go for brunch or lunch and enjoy savory quiche, croque monsieur, artisanal petite baguette sandwiches, or smoked salmon croissants. Be sure to leave room for dessert, where Chef Feret truly shines, with almost-too-stunning-to-eat creations. With two locations, it's easy to take a bite out of France.

17 Harbourside Ln., Hilton Head Island, 843-715-3349
1018 William Hilton Pkwy., Hilton Head Island, 843-715-2598
hiltonheadsocialbakery.com

3

GET YOUR VEGGIE ON
AT HERBAN MARKET & CAFE

Beaufort's only veg-centric restaurant, Herban Market & Cafe, serves up herbaceous and delicious food for breakfast, brunch, lunch, and midday pick-me-ups, and has won over not only herbivores, but carnivores and omnivores alike. Featuring a robust coffee and tea menu; healthy (and tasty) juices and smoothies; sumptuous scratch-made daily baked goods, including artisan breads, classic croissants, and luscious pastries; and hot breakfast options, like the Herban breakfast croissant (egg, avocado, tomato, spinach, and Havarti cheese on a house-made croissant), breakfast burrito, or vegetarian biscuits and "sausage" gravy. Lunch offerings highlight sandwich standards done vegan-style, including a smoky beet Reuben, a house-made veggie burger, a BLT with tempeh bacon and Vegenaise, and a falafel wrap. Naturally, they offer some uber-healthy and delicious salad options, along with creative desserts like blackberry goat cheese cheesecake, beetroot cupcakes, and avocado brownies. Dining is available inside or alfresco, with views of the Beaufort River.

1601 North St., Beaufort, 843-379-5060
herbanmarketandcafe.com

4

QUENCH YOUR THIRST
AT BURNT CHURCH DISTILLERY

You'll find world-class spirits and much more at bustling and beautiful Burnt Church Distillery in Bluffton, including tours, classes, varied themed flights, and creative cocktails created with their house-made spirits. The possibilities include bourbon, whiskey, rye whiskey, bourbon cream, vodka, gin, and flavored moonshines, like iced coffee, chocolate milk, and sweet potato pie. But the food is also a big draw. The menu features creative appetizers and salads, pasta, pizzas, and tacos, and there's also beer and wine, non-alcoholic cocktails, cigars, and a unique collection of Lowcountry-leaning and branded merchandise. The cathedral-like setting, including stunning stained glass, makes it easy to join the Burnt Church congregation. Tours should be booked in advance. Burnt Church Distillery is one of many successful Lowcountry offerings from Moon King Entertainment Group, including The Bank, Side Hustle Brewing Company, and the Ma Daisy's Porch complex (where you will find the Bluffton Gullah Cultural Heritage Center).

120 Bluffton Rd., Bluffton, 843-872-0158
burntchurchdistillery.com

TIP

The Bank (thebankhhi.com), near Coligny Circle on Hilton Head Island, is a beer garden and so much more, with three bars, six eateries, live entertainment, activities and games, and a retail shop.

OTHER LOWCOUNTRY PLACES TO GET YOUR SPIRIT ON

Daufuskie Island Distillery

270 Haig Point Rd., Daufuskie Island, 843-342-4786
daufuskierum.com

Hilton Head Distillery

14 Cardinal Rd., Hilton Head Island, 843-686-4443
hiltonheaddistillery.com

Lucky Duck Distillery

17B Yemassee Hwy., Yemassee, 843-589-5440
luckyduckdistillery.com

Rotten Little Bastard Distillery

2139 Boundary St., Ste. 102, Beaufort, 843-379-5252
rottenlittlebastarddistillery.com

Shinetown Moonshine

857 James L. Taylor Rd., Ridgeland, 843-645-0657
facebook.com/shinetownmoonshineandwine

FEED YOUR HUNGER
AT ROXBURY MERCANTILE

Conveniently located on the Edisto Island National Scenic Byway, Roxbury Mercantile is a culinary outpost that's a nostalgic throwback to the small town mom-and-pop restaurants of yesteryear. Situated on the Barnwell family farm, the original Roxbury Mercantile was an old country store that served the Edisto Island and St. Paul's Parish communities for nearly eight decades, before it tragically burned down in 1983. Today, co-owners William "Beau" Barnwell, a 10th generation Lowcountry native, and his wife, Jackie, who grew up on Hilton Head Island, have reimagined Roxbury Mercantile as a restaurant specializing in Southern hospitality, craft cocktails, and classic Lowcountry cuisine. The uncomplicated menu relies heavily on local and regional farmers and fishers to produce crowd favorites, such as their bourbon butter shrimp and grits, lightly cornmeal-battered fried seafood, juicy grass-fed beef burgers, fried green tomato tacos, and more.

4398 Hwy. 174, Meggett, 843-889-0044
roxburymercantile.com

6

DINE IN A MANSION
AT RIBAUT SOCIAL CLUB

Tucked inside Beaufort's elegant antebellum mansion Anchorage 1770, a premier boutique inn on Beaufort's Bay Street, the intimate Ribaut Social Club is one of the area's finest white tablecloth restaurants, making for a perfectly romantic date night or special occasion meal. Named for a men's club that was started in the house by a former owner in 1891, the restaurant is a throwback to the spirit and atmosphere of the original Ribaut Social Club. It features creative cuisine, along with a sophisticated wine list curated by co-owner Amy Lesesne. The limited menu offers impeccable regional fare, like crispy brussels sprouts with a Korean butter glaze and seasonal salads for starters, plus reinvented entrees like duck a l'orange, chicken marsala, and a to-die-for 16-ounce Certified Angus ribeye. Dinner is served on the main floor and the massive front porch of the tabby mansion, with stunning Beaufort River and marina views.

1103 Bay St., Beaufort, 843-525-1770
ribautsocialclub.com

TIP

If time permits, book a room at Anchorage 1770 (anchorage1770.com) and spend the night. Inn guests can enjoy cocktails on one of the two grand verandas overlooking Bay Street and the Beaufort River, dinner at Ribaut Social Club, and even breakfast in bed the next morning.

7

EAT EVERYTHING BUT THE OINK

AT RIZER'S PORK & PRODUCE

Offering varied country-style all-you-can-eat comfort food buffets for lunch from Wednesday to Saturday, Rizer's Pork & Produce features pork, produce, and more from the Rizer family farm and beyond. Wednesday's buffet is smaller than the other days, while Thursday boasts a full buffet, but no seafood. Fridays and Saturdays bring a full buffet that includes fish and shrimp, plus dessert, like homemade pound cake, a scoop of ice cream (four flavors), or banana pudding. Buffet highlights typically include several entree choices, like Rizer's sausage and barbecue in their secret sauce, and lots of country-style side dishes, including various vegetables, classic macaroni and cheese, and more. Plus, their bi-weekly steak nights (January to August) feature 16-ounce steaks, blooming onions, hot rolls, huge baked potatoes, a long list of side vegetables (choose two), and the same friendly Rizer's vibe and service.

2357 Confederate Hwy., Lodge, 843-866-2645
rizersporkandproduce.com

TIP

Like a farm market, Rizer's Pork & Produce also offers a large selection of fresh pork products, including their famous made-in-store sausage and pretty much everything else but the oink. There's also seasonal produce from their farm, with a wide variety of beans and peas, sweet corn, watermelons, greens, and much more.

8

OBEY THE URGE TO DINE

AT SERG RESTAURANTS

Back in 1984, Hilton Head Island was hungry for a neighborhood pizzeria experience, and high school and college buddies Steve Carb and Tony Arcuri—serious pizza lovers who had eaten their way through Pittsburgh's many renowned pizza joints—were happy to say, "Si!" to the concept. With the help of partner Rick Meccariello, Giuseppi's Pizza & Pasta House opened on the island. Fellow college roommate and trusted friend Jim Loniero was brought in as a partner soon after the company was founded, and the rest is SERG (Southeast Entertainment Restaurant Group) history. Today, SERG's award-winning family of restaurants and concepts numbers 18 (and counting), including landmark Skull Creek Boathouse, as well as Poseidon, WiseGuys, CharBar Co., Nectar, and their unique takeaway spot, SERG Takeout Kitchen. The SERG family of restaurants now offers a wide variety of cuisines, including seafood, Italian American, modern American, burgers, sushi, farm-to-table fare, barbecue, and even a brewery.

serggroup.com

9

TASTE THE SEA
AT LOCALS RAW BAR

Showcasing sea-to-table fare, Locals Raw Bar on Lady's Island wows locals and visitors alike with their creative takes on raw seafood, Asian fusion specialties, and creative sushi. Owned and operated by local husband-and-wife team Hunter and Jessie Cozart, the pair took a leap of faith when an iconic restaurant location became available. Open for lunch, dinner, and brunch, Locals serves "soulful Japanese," according to Hunter, with small plates like steam buns, Not So Clear soup (chicken dashi with chicken and shrimp dumplings), and local oysters. Big plates include poke bowls (along with several other creative bowls); lobster rolls; lobster grilled cheese; smashburgers; shellfish fried rice; stunning sushi rolls with tuna, crab, and local fish, like rudderfish and porgy; and okonomiyaki (a very popular cabbage pancake). The drinks menu is impressive, including well-paired sakes and creative cocktails.

97 Sea Island Pkwy., Beaufort, 843-379-9348
localsrawbar.com

10

DIVE DEEPLY INTO SOUTHERN COOKING

AT BUCKY'S SEAFOOD

What started with Walterboro native Willie J. "Bucky" Williams selling seafood out of a gray Ford pickup truck and then opening Williams Seafood has evolved into a very popular Walterboro restaurant, where the slogan is, "Deep Southern Cooking." Serving breakfast, lunch, and dinner, and featuring so much more than seafood, Bucky's Seafood has to be experienced multiple times to be fully appreciated. Breakfast at Bucky's means eggs offered six ways; varied seafood (think whiting, bream, croaker, salmon patties, scallops, shrimp, oysters, and more); meats (from sausage to bologna to Southern breakfast liver pudding, which is sometimes called scrapple); and pancakes. For lunch and dinner, the extensive possibilities include varied seafood dinners, combos, baskets, fillets, and sandwiches; snow crab legs; beloved garlic blue crabs; popular soul food dinners; "land items"; and more than a dozen Lowcountry-leaning Southern sides (think collards, fried okra, yams, grits, and more). There's a kids' menu, homemade desserts, and a full bar.

1208 Hampton St., Walterboro, 843-549-5917
buckysseafood.com

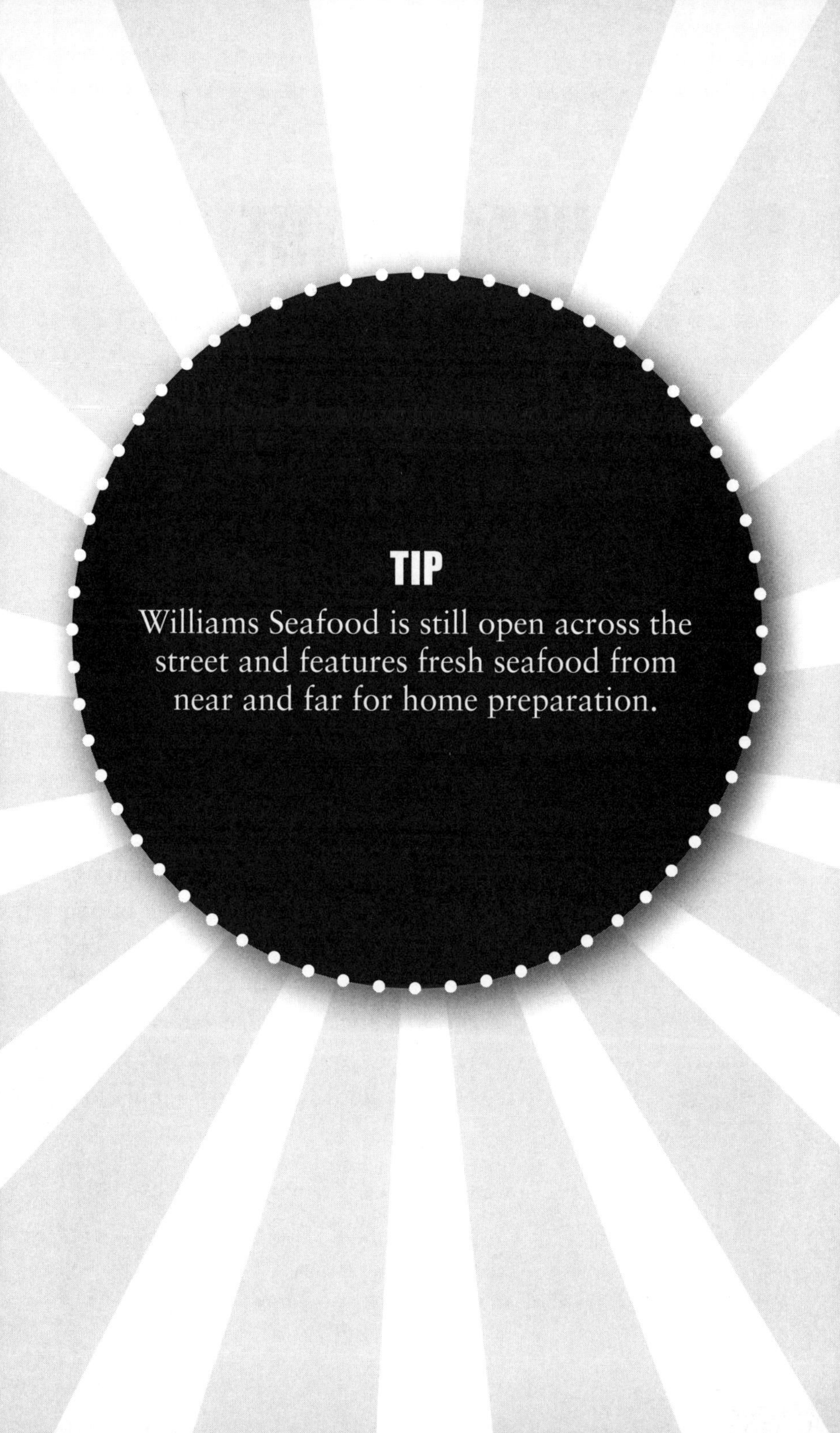
TIP
Williams Seafood is still open across the street and features fresh seafood from near and far for home preparation.

11

HEAD TO THE COUNTRYSIDE FOR COUNTRY COOKIN'

AT HAROLD'S COUNTRY CLUB

Originally a Chevy dealership and then a garage and gas station run by Harold Peeples, locals began gathering at Harold's in Yemassee as far back as the 1970s for Thursday night potluck suppers. That evolved into the garage area becoming a restaurant and bar that opens several nights a week for themed dinners amongst a collection of unique relics and a convivial atmosphere. Thursday nights are still potluck night (with the schedule including fried pork chops, fried chicken and gizzards, or barbecue pork & hash), with a menu on Friday night featuring wings, seafood, hamburgers, and more, and steaks on Saturdays, where you reserve your steak (along with all the fixings) at one of two seating times. Sweet iced tea and longneck beers are the beverages of choice, though wine drinkers will love the five-buck corkage fee. Harold's Country Club is located in close proximity to four Lowcountry counties, so its motto is, "In the middle of nowhere, but close to everywhere."

97 US Hwy. 21 (97 Lowcountry Hwy.), Yemassee, 843-589-4360
haroldscountryclub.com

12

SAVOR A BEAUFORT TRIFECTA

AT PLUMS, SALTUS, AND HEARTH

Local restaurateur Lantz Price has been feeding the community for decades at a trifecta of restaurants along Bay Street in Beaufort. The original is Plums, showcasing casual Lowcountry cuisine and specialties featuring local ingredients and flavors, including pimento cheese, shrimp salad BLT, smoked gouda mac and cheese, po boys, Lowcountry gumbo, and shrimp and grits, all with a river view. Saltus River Grill offers elevated Lowcountry cuisine in a historic building, with nods to its past and one of the city's best riverfront patios. Open for dinner only, the menu at Saltus features specialties like shellfish towers, a signature crab bisque, crab cakes, diver scallops, osso buco, chargrilled steaks, fresh market catch, and a full sushi and sashimi menu. And, lastly, Hearth Wood Fired Pizza serves creative pizzas, meatballs, meat and cheese boards, Italian heroes and sandwiches, antipasto, Italian salads, and heaping pastas in a woodsy fish camp meets surf camp meets Italian trattoria space.

Plums
904 Bay St., Beaufort, 843-525-1946
plumsrestaurant.com

Saltus River Grill
802 Bay St., Beaufort, 843-379-3474
saltusrivergrill.com

Hearth Wood Fired Pizza
802 Bay St., Beaufort, 843-379-9806
hearthpizzabft.com

13

LEARN TO COOK

AT THE CULINARY INSTITUTE OF THE SOUTH

Where better to learn how to cook than at a culinary institute? Bluffton's Culinary Institute of the South at the Technical College of the Lowcountry (TCL) makes learning to cook easy, with a Personal Enrichment program targeted to food enthusiasts who are looking to expand their knowledge. Featuring three-hour immersive and entertaining hands-on classes from chefs, culinary experts, and guest instructors in state-of-the-art kitchens, guests learn kitchen basics, knife tips, and cooking terminology, all while whipping up a tasty meal to enjoy at the end of class. If dining is preferred over cooking, head to the campus for a cup of coffee and a grab-and-go pastry at Clist Café, or enjoy a multicourse lunch at The Bistro and let TCL's culinary, baking, and pastry arts students cook for you as part of their curriculum. Be sure to leave time to explore the Foodseum, an interactive deep dive into the Lowcountry's culinary history and agricultural impact on the dining world.

1 Venture Dr., Bluffton, 843-305-8575
tcl.edu/culinary-institute

Since The Bistro is run by students working as chefs and servers, it is open seasonally when classes are in session. Be sure to check the website for open days and hours. The Clist Café is open Monday to Thursday from 9 a.m. to 3 p.m.

14

COAST ON OVER

TO BENNY'S COASTAL KITCHEN

Part of the popular multi-restaurant Coastal Restaurants and Bars (CRAB) group, Benny's Coastal Kitchen overlooking Skull Creek opened in 2024 to rave reviews and has been coasting along with its many new and veteran fans ever since. With some of Hilton Head Island's best water views and sunsets, plus seasonally driven seafood-leaning menus to match, Benny's has become a Hilton Head Island favorite. The lunch menu typically includes local May River oysters, famed oyster bisque, light bites (including sinful hush puppies), handhelds (like their grouper sandwich), and more. Dinner brings more oysters and bisque, an array of appetizers (including "The Perch," which features chilled scampi clams, shucked oysters, poached shrimp, and Alaskan snow crab legs), salads, and creative "Benny's Bounty" entrees. There are also delectable desserts, Sunday brunch, and the 41 UP rooftop bar, which is a sunset hotspot. The name "Benny's" is a tribute to Benny Hudson, a legendary figure in the local seafood industry. Benny Hudson Seafood (bennyhudsonseafood.com) retail market is nearby.

75 Shrimpers Row, Hilton Head Island, 843-715-2202
bennyshiltonhead.com

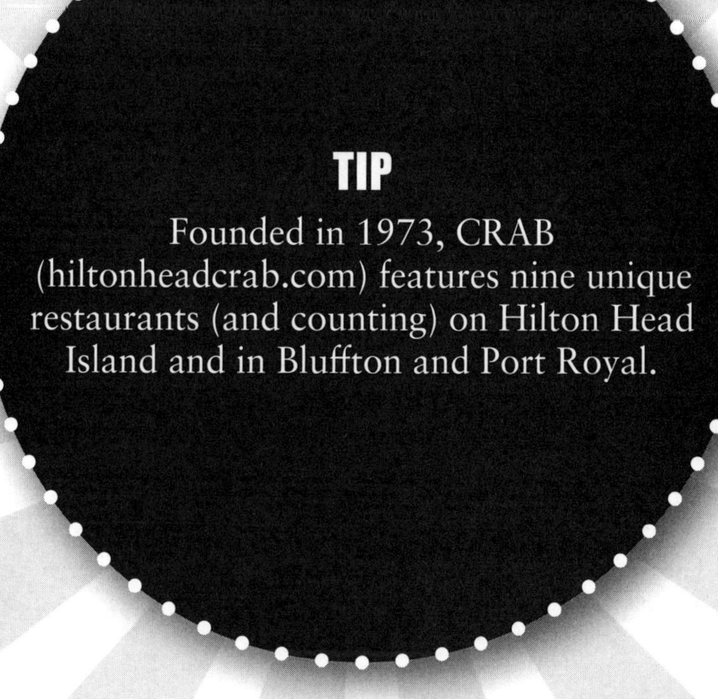

TIP

Founded in 1973, CRAB (hiltonheadcrab.com) features nine unique restaurants (and counting) on Hilton Head Island and in Bluffton and Port Royal.

15

SUPPORT LOCAL FARMERS
AT LOWCOUNTRY FARMERS MARKETS

Farmers markets across the country are hotter than a scotch bonnet pepper. They help local farmers sell the fruits (and veggies) of their labor; give home cooks and chefs access to fresh, nutritious, and local food; and create a vital community connection. Fortunately, the Lowcountry has an abundance of flavorful farmers markets to choose from, all showcasing farmers and artisans of vegetables, fruits, grains, meats, seafood, dairy, plants, juices, and coffees and teas, along with vendors selling a variety of prepared foods and baked goods. The Port Royal Farmers Market can be found at Naval Heritage Park on Saturdays year-round; Tuesdays feature the Farmers Market of Hilton Head year-round at the Coastal Discovery Museum, and the Farmers & Makers Market at The Shops at Sea Pines Center from March to November; and the Farmers Market of Bluffton happens on Thursdays year-round at Martin Family Park in historic downtown Bluffton.

Port Royal Farmers Market
1615 Ribaut Rd., Port Royal
portroyalfarmersmarket.com

Farmers Market of Hilton Head
70 Honey Horn Dr.,
Hilton Head Island
coastaldiscovery.org/explore/events/farmers-market

Farmers & Makers Market
71 Lighthouse Rd.,
Hilton Head Island
theshopsatseapinescenter.com

Farmers Market of Bluffton
68 Boundary St., Bluffton
farmersmarketbluffton.org

OTHER AREA FARMERS MARKETS

Colleton Museum & Farmers Market

Saturdays, May to December; Tuesdays, year-round

506 E Washington St., Walterboro, 843-549-2303
colletonmuseum.org/farmers-market

George & Pink's

Daily year-round

7971 Eddingsville Beach Rd., Edisto Island, 843-869-2425

King's Farm Market

Daily year-round

2559 Hwy. 174, Edisto Island, 843-869-3600
kingsfarmmarket.com

Town of Ridgeland Farmers Market

Fridays and Saturdays, April to December

7753 W Main St., Ridgeland
ridgelandsc.gov/town-of-ridgeland-farmers-market

Barefoot Farms

Daily year-round

939 Sea Island Pkwy., St. Helena Island, 843-838-7421

Dempsey Farms

Harvesting dates vary; check their
website for dates and hours

1576 Sea Island Pkwy., St. Helena Island, 843-838-3656
dempseyfarmsupick.com

16

SAY CHEERS
TO SHELLRING ALEWORKS

Situated in Port Royal's former shrimp processing plant and featuring a welcoming vibe and hip interior, plus a bustling outdoor space with seating and great views, waterfront Shellring Aleworks is a great addition to the Lowcountry food, beverage, and music scenes. The beer list changes weekly, and the possibilities include a variety of IPAs for hopheads; their malty Shellinator; several sours; "Lite" pours, like the Nautical Light 98 (aka "Naughty Lite"), which is perfect for the Lowcountry lifestyle; and many more. Beers are generally available in 5-, 10-, and 16-ounce pours and also in six-packs or in a growler, as well as a "Flight of Four" 5-ounce pours. First-time visitors and veteran Shellringers go for the world-class beers, a great wine list, creative grub, and of course, the lush views. But they also head there for varied live music, which has become a huge hit with locals and visitors alike.

1111 11th St., Port Royal, 843-379-2370
shellringaleworks.com

TIP

Often found in the Lowcountry and elsewhere on the South Carolina, Georgia, and Florida coastlines, Indigenous shell rings are typically circular deposits of shell and more.

GET FISHY
AT ACE BASIN FISH CAMP

It seems fitting that the Lowcountry would have an old school fish camp-style restaurant offering out in the countryside. Open Wednesday to Saturday for lunch and dinner, and supper only on Sunday, ACE Basin Fish Camp's lunch and dinner menus include specials with coleslaw, hush puppies, and a side choice, including the popular "pick two" combo platter, where you make the difficult decision between shrimp, scallops, oysters, clam strips, and fish. There's also whole flounder, crab cakes, other varied fish, and other sandwiches, including oyster and shrimp po boys. There are other tasty platters, varied lobster feasts, and lots of other entrees come supper time. Of course, non-fishy folks will find steaks, burgers, chicken, and more on the menus, as well. The family-friendly restaurant on US 17 boasts a great atmosphere and service that's anything but fishy or campy.

16503 Ace Basin Pkwy., Jacksonboro, 843-893-3474
facebook.com/acebasinfishcamp

TIP

Fish camp fans will also love CRAB restaurant group's Fishcamp on 11th Street (fishcampon11th.com) in Port Royal and Hilton Head Island's Fishcamp on Broad Creek (fishcamphhi.com).

18

EAT FARM-TO-FORK
AT FARM

Long-time fans of FARM Hospitality Group executive chef Brandon Carter's cooking know him from his days at nearby Palmetto Bluff. Today, beloved FARM pays homage to the bounty of the Lowcountry in a rustic chic farmhouse setting in bustling Old Town Bluffton. Carter (a South Carolina Chef Ambassador) and his team show the love to local farmers, fishermen, and artisan producers and suppliers with a menu that combines unique flavor combinations with what's fresh. Whether it's the burrata, ham, peach, and arugula starter; shrimp risotto; or grilled flounder with pattypan squash and leeks, the highly composed and very shareable plates are elevated, yet familiar and comforting. FARM really shines when it comes to local vegetables from area farms. Chef Carter and his kitchen team also rule the roost with local seafood and meats. There's a great view of the open kitchen, as well as a popular bar, and a private dining room upstairs.

1301 May River Rd., Bluffton, 843-707-2041
farmbluffton.com

TIP

Carter and his partners also have four tasty options in Savannah: Common Thread, Strange Bird, Flora and Fauna, and Wildflower Cafe on Telfair Square.

19

HEAD TO
HUDSON'S SEAFOOD HOUSE ON THE DOCKS

For a classic Lowcountry seafood meal at one of Hilton Head Island's oldest restaurants, it's a long-time tradition to head to the docks on Skull Creek in Port Royal Sound for a fresh-from-the-docks choice of seafood and more at Hudson's Seafood House on the Docks. A legendary Lowcountry restaurant since 1967 and located in a former 1920 seafood processing plant, heading to Hudson's means fresh seafood that's steamed, fried, pan-seared, blackened, or broiled, as well as fresh oysters they grow and harvest (Shell Ring Oyster Company). But the extensive menus feature much more, including she crab soup and gumbo; fried green tomatoes; a "Can't Decide" briny appetizers sampler; Lowcountry boils and other seafood-focused combos; their beefy brisket burger and other meat lover options; homemade desserts; and more, like the beloved fried oyster Benedict for Sunday brunch. There's casual seating inside, as well as outside on the water, where there's a lively bar, convivial vibe, and classic Skull Creek sunsets.

1 Hudson Rd., Hilton Head Island, 843-681-2772
hudsonsonthedocks.com

20

FEAST ON
FINGER-LICKIN' FRIED CHICKEN

There are lots of Lowcountry hotspots for Southern fried chicken (and other fried foods, like local seafood and vegetables), including Cahill's Market & Chicken Kitchen in Bluffton; Beaufort's Maryland Fried Chicken and Q's Chicken Shack; and Rigdon's Fried Chicken in Hampton. However, conveniently located Hardeeville Chiken Lickn, just off I-95 in Hardeeville, remains a favorite for fried chicken lovers near and far. The menu starts with their famed two-piece fried chicken, plus a choice of one, two, or three tasty sides. There are lots of other chicken options (like tenders, livers, gizzards, smoked, and wingettes); fried fish; two-, three-, and even four-meat combos with two sides; daily specials; mixed chicken boxes; and more. You order inside and dive right in at one of the tables out front or get it to go, which is very popular with locals and hungry road warriors passing through.

16161 Whyte Hardee Blvd., Hardeeville, 843-784-9415
hardeevillechikenlickn.com

OTHER TOP LOWCOUNTRY CHOICES FOR FRIED CHICKEN

Cahill's Market & Chicken Kitchen

1055 May River Rd., Bluffton, 843-757-2921
cahillsmarket.com

Maryland Fried Chicken

111 Ribaut Rd., Beaufort, 843-524-8766
mfc-beaufort.com

Q's Chicken Shack

40 Sea Island Pkwy., Beaufort, 843-379-7757
qschickenshack.com

Rigdon's Fried Chicken

801 Magnolia St. W, Hampton, 803-943-4383

ENJOY BREAKFAST, BRUNCH, OR LUNCH
AT MAGNOLIA CAFE

Serving breakfast and lunch all day, Beaufort's Magnolia Cafe menu is a "greatest hits" of breakfast, brunch, and lunch options. The extensive menu features toasts (although the avocado is one of their biggest sellers, don't overlook the stunning whipped ricotta); egg sandwiches with spinach and tomato on house-made English muffins; a breakfast bowl with scrambled eggs, chorizo (or tofu), cheese, salsa, black beans, avocado, and home fries; frittatas; waffles; house-made soups; hearty entree salads (like the 3-Salad Plate and grilled pecan chicken salad); lunch rice bowls with varied toppings; and creative sandwiches like chicken caprese or grilled vegetables with pesto and Boursin cheese. They also feature an extensive take-away coffee (King Bean Coffee out of Charleston) and tea (Hale Tea Co. out of Savannah) menu as you enter, along with a case of delectable scones, muffins, cinnamon rolls, and more.

703 Congress St., Beaufort, 843-816-8535
magnoliabeaufort.com

TIP

Magnolia Cafe's owners also own and operate Bluffton's delectable Downtown Deli and Downtown Catering.

downtowncateringcompany.com

SEE THE UGLY FISH
AT WHALEY'S

Founded in 1948 and once an island gas station and convenience store, Whaley's Restaurant & Bar is an Edisto Beach and Lowcountry classic for good reason. Known as the "Home of the Ugly Fish" (be sure to ask a server to point it out), Whaley's has a *Sanford and Son* vibe, with lunch and dinner menus that have something for seafood lovers and landlubbers alike. "Whaley's Classics" on both menus include their famed crab cake starter, sushi nachos (featuring pan-seared ahi tuna), and shrimp-and-crab bisque, while the lunch menu's classic "Sammiches" add a crab cake sandwich and the Sarah Jane BLT (with grilled shrimp), as well as very popular lunch specials. Dinner-only possibilities include crab cakes and shrimp and grits featuring fresh local shrimp. The wings and burgers are also popular with Whaley's veterans and first-timers alike. The often-bustling bar provides a great place to meet locals, as well as a perfect perch for a drink, snack, or meal.

2801 Myrtle St., Edisto Beach, 843-869-2161
whaleyseb.com

23

DRINK AND EAT WELL
AT BLACKSHEEP X SABBATICAL

Beloved Lowcountry chef extraordinaire Matt Wallace and GM and sommelier Krista Duffy have crafted a Beaufort wine and food experience unlike anything in the Lowcountry and beyond. After developing a huge following as a unique tasting menu restaurant simply called Blacksheep, it has evolved into a no-reservations wine and food destination called Blacksheep X Sabbatical. With a motto of, "Wine Always, Food Sometimes," this ever-evolving food and drink luncheonette-style hotspot and wine shop features counter service for ordering wine and, likely, food. Wallace's creative concoctions include his creamy caramelized onion dip; colorful salads using fresh seasonal produce, legumes, and unique tinned seafood (like grilled octopus and more); and unusual sandwiches (typically served on ciabatta). Duffy will help with perfect wine pairings, as well as simply recommending a stand-alone glass or a bottle to enjoy there or later. They also offer popular takeout (including online or in-house ordering), wine tastings, and oft-booked private dinners.

1216 Boundary St., Beaufort, 843-470-8070
blacksheeponboundary.com

TIP

Blacksheep veterans often start their visit with a "pony" bottle of Miller High Life or "picnic" bloody mary to whet their appetites.

24

TAKE A TASTE
OF COTTAGE LIFE

Combining creative cuisine with Southern hospitality and shopping for baked goods, tea, and more, the Cottage Café, Bakery & Tea Room in Old Town Bluffton is one of the Lowcountry's tastiest and most tasteful destinations. The building that houses the Cottage was built in 1868 by J. J. Carson, who is known for saving General Stonewall Jackson's life during the Civil War battle of Chancellorsville. Today, chef/owner Leslie Rohland (a South Carolina Chef Ambassador) oversees the popular eatery and shop. Her breakfast, lunch, and Sunday brunch menus feature flavorful takes on Lowcountry favorites, including lots of egg options (from Cottage corned beef hash to crabby Benedicts); shrimp and grits; tomato pie; crab cakes; and much more. They also serve afternoon teas. Post-meal shoppers will love the Cottage Café's huge selection of teas and baked goods, as well as other tasty offerings from the Lowcountry, like Edisto's Marsh Hen Mill heirloom grits and more.

38 Calhoun St., Bluffton, 843-757-0508
thecottagebluffton.com

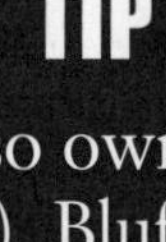

Chef Roland also owns the Juice Hive (thejuicehive.com), Bluffton Pasta Shoppe (blufftonpastashoppe.com), and May River Coffee Roasters (mayrivercoffeeroasters.com), which are all in Bluffton as well.

25

EAT TASTY COASTAL 'CUE
IN THE LOWCOUNTRY

The South Carolina Barbecue Trail leads the way to world-class barbecue in the Lowcountry. Featuring many varied barbecue styles, sauces, meats, and stops—from Estill to Beaufort and Port Royal and down to Bluffton and Hilton Head Island—it's easy to find tasty 'cue in the Lowcountry.

discoversouthcarolina.com/barbecue

Head to the countryside for mouthwatering BBQ:

Dukes Barbecue
949 Robertson Blvd., Walterboro, 843-549-1446
dukes-barbecue.res-menu.com

Duke's BBQ
10190 S Jacob Smart Blvd., Ridgeland, 843-726-6244
facebook.com/dukessc

Lester's Country BBQ
8500 Savannah Hwy., Estill, 803-625-2305
facebook.com/lesterscountrybbq

Pistol Jo's Cherry Point BBQ
2915 Okatie Hwy., Ridgeland, 843-645-4227
facebook.com/cherrypointbbq

BEAUFORT & PORT ROYAL BBQ

Q on Bay

822 Bay St., Beaufort, 843-524-7771
qonbay.com

Roadhouse

7 Toppers Ln., Port Royal, 843-379-8899
roadhouseribs.com

The Smokehouse at Paris Avenue

914 Paris Ave., Port Royal, 843-522-0322
thesmokehouseatparisavenue.com

BLUFFTON & HILTON HEAD ISLAND BBQ

Bluffton BBQ

11 State of Mind St., Bluffton, 843-757-7427
facebook.com/blufftonbbq

Bullies BBQ

3 Regency Pkwy., Hilton Head Island, 843-686-7427
bulliesbbq.com

Choo Choo BBQ

129 Burnt Church Rd., Bluffton, 843-815-7675
choochoobbq.net

Forrest Fire BBQ

1 N Forest Beach Dr., Hilton Head Island, 843-341-3473
forrestfirehhi.com

One Hot Mama's

104 Buckwalter Pkwy., Ste. 1A, Bluffton, 843-815-6262
35 Office Park Rd., Hilton Head Island, 843-682-6262
onehotmamas.com

The Smokehouse

34 Palmetto Bay Rd., Hilton Head Island, 843-842-4227
smokehousehhi.com

Daily live music at Tiki Hut
Courtesy of Navadise Media

MUSIC AND ENTERTAINMENT

ENJOY DAILY LIVE MUSIC YEAR-ROUND
AT TIKI HUT

Since 1977, Hilton Head Island's iconic Tiki Hut has been one of the Lowcountry's top places to enjoy live music every day of the year. Situated on Coligny Beach and greatly expanded and enhanced in 2024, Tiki Hut is located at popular Beach House Hilton Head Island resort. The impressive schedule of live music includes two or three acts a day, with varied jam sessions from talented musicians typically leading to lots of dancing and rounds of ice-cold beers and cocktails. Along with those popular beverages, there's a full menu for lunch, dinner, and weekend brunch. Lunch and dinner "Intros" include Buffalo chicken fries and house-made chili, with "Chorus" options including their bacon smashburger (with American Wagyu beef), blackened mahi and jerk chicken sandwiches, a huge footlong chili cheese dog, and more. Brunch brings an "Early Burger," with pork sausage and Wagyu beef, and lots of other tasty brunch choices, like the blackened mahi omelet.

1 S Forest Beach Dr., Hilton Head Island, 843-785-5126
tikihuthhi.com

TIP

Serious music (and Tiki Hut) fans should consider basing themselves at adjacent Beach House Hilton Head Island (beachhousehhi.com), where the beach vibe continues.

SUPPORT ALL THE ARTS
AT THE CENTER FOR THE ARTS

It's no surprise that a college town would have an arts center that is a theater, entertainment venue, movie theater, art museum, and classroom all rolled into one. And that's exactly what you'll find at the University of South Carolina Beaufort's Center for the Arts. Featuring a full season of shows from September through May, including production musicals and dramas, varied music from vocalists to bands to musical tributes, and children's shows, the Center for the Arts also shows feature films on their (Occasional) Monday Night Movies; is the home to USCB Chamber Music; offers art classes like Rag Rug; and features authors, musicians, and storytellers at Listen on the Lawn. Throughout the year, the Center also hosts art shows and installations, as well as various events, including the Pat Conroy Literary Festival, the Beaufort International Film Festival, Books Sandwiched In, and the Lunch with Authors series.

805 Carteret St., Beaufort, 843-521-4145
uscbcenterforthearts.com

28

CELEBRATE HOLLYWOOD IN HAMPTON

AT THE PALMETTO THEATER

Located on Lee Avenue in the heart of rural Hampton, the county seat of Hampton County, the Palmetto Theater is an Art Deco architectural beacon breathing life into the revitalized downtown. Built in 1946 in the Art Moderne style, the theater features a prominent and ornate semi-circle protruding marquee with colorful neon lettering and geometric design. Built with a stage for live performances and originally seating 450 people, the venue was once the social center of the community. A working theater through the 1970s and 1980s, times changed and the theater fell on hard times. Now owned and operated by the nonprofit Hampton Friends of the Arts, the theater has undergone an interior refurbishment (creating a more intimate experience with only 200 seats) and the installation of state-of-the-art digital projection and sound. Hosting movies, theatrical performances, concerts, and art exhibits in their new "Palmetto Gallery" lobby, the Palmetto Theater is once again welcoming guests with old-world theater charm.

109 Lee Ave., Hampton, 803-842-9842
palmettotheater.org

29

SPLASH INTO
THE BEAUFORT WATER FESTIVAL

With a region that is surrounded by marshlands, waterways, creeks, rivers, and an ocean, it's no surprise that there would be an event to celebrate Beaufort's briny bounty. At least that's what a group of friends thought in the 1950s when they created the Beaufort Water Festival as a way to highlight Beaufort's fun on the water. What began as a two-weekend event with boat races, a beauty pageant, and dances has expanded into a 10-day, all-volunteer celebration featuring raft races, a toad fishing tournament, shrimp boat displays, a waterskiing show, an air show, a parade, concerts, a Lowcountry supper, a craft market, fireworks, and a Blessing of the Fleet and boat parade to close out the celebration. Every July since 1956, the festival has drawn tens of thousands of people from other parts of the state, as well as the country, and Beaufort transforms into a massive stage for an unforgettable outdoor celebration.

Henry C. Chambers Waterfront Park, Bay St., Beaufort, 843-524-0600
bftwaterfestival.com

TIP

Parking is at a premium in downtown Beaufort during the festival. Plan on taking the shuttle from the Beaufort County Government Center and leave the parking to others. Bring chairs, but leave your coolers at home.

LISTEN UP

AT THE JAZZ CORNER

Since 1999, the Jazz Corner on Hilton Head Island has been a Lowcountry "must-do" for locals and visitors alike. Of course, people come for the world-class music, but they stay (and come back) for much more, including the vibe, the company of like-minded listeners, the staff and service, and last, but definitely not least, the Jazz Corner's delectable dining. Bob and Lois Masteller envisioned opening a jazz club with the esteemed George Shearing Quintet, and the jazz icon agreed to perform opening week. Their dream continues decades later, with the Jazz Corner featuring regional artists Sunday through Thursday and touring regional, national, and international artists Fridays and Saturdays. Lois and her son, David, continue the legacy, with David joining the Jazz Corner Ensemble onstage most Tuesday evenings. Food also remains a huge draw to the intimate setting, thanks to a creative menu of appetizers, entrees, and desserts, plus interesting wines and cocktails.

1000 William Hilton Pkwy., C-1, Hilton Head Island, 843-842-8620
thejazzcorner.com

TIP

Reservations are highly recommended.

SEE A SHOW
AT THE ARTS CENTER OF COASTAL CAROLINA

The largest equity theater in the state, the Arts Center of Coastal Carolina produces five shows each season, including musicals, dramas, and comedies, with every production element created in-house, from casting and rehearsal to set construction and costume design. Talent is auditioned in New York, resulting in top-notch performers, many of whom have appeared on Broadway. The Arts Center also presents other world-class performances throughout the year, including comedians, contemporary musical groups, jazz performers, international dance companies, illusionists, and more, along with free outdoor festivals like the Town's Holiday Kick-Off Festival and Voices of Gullah. Dynamic educational programs are offered for all ages year-round, including visual and performance art workshops, lectures, and field trips, as well as displays of youth and educational art throughout the state-of-the-art center.

14 Shelter Cove Ln., Hilton Head Island, 843-842-2787
artshhi.com

TAKE IN A PERFORMANCE

AT COLLETON CIVIC CENTER AND HAMPTON ST. AUDITORIUM

Historic Colleton Civic Center and Hampton St. Auditorium is Colleton County's premier event space for many arts and civic activities in downtown Walterboro. The old converted school is now a popular, county-run facility with studio space for various artists, as well as classes, workshops, and a variety of groups and activities. Two main spaces in the building that are utilized by the community, as well as renters, include the art gallery/multipurpose room (showcasing artwork from around the area and region) and the updated 480-seat Hampton St. Auditorium. Traveling groups rent the auditorium to bring in shows and performances, as well as the Civic Center hosting varied shows, performances, comedy, workshops, and more, including the annual WHAM! Festival (Walterboro History, Art, and Music Festival). The historic building has also been the setting for filming in major motion pictures, including *Forrest Gump* and *Radio*.

494 Hampton St., Walterboro, 843-549-8360
colletoncivic.org

GO TO THE MOVIES
WITH BEAUFORT TOURS

The Lowcountry has seen its share of filmmaking over the years, with many area locations standing in for fictional and real places like Greenbow, Alabama; Ravenel, South Carolina; and Vietnam. A great way to see these film locations is to book a tour with Beaufort Tours. Tour participants will see the Gump Medical Center and the bridge that Tom Hanks crosses on the way back from his cross-country run in *Forrest Gump*; the house where former classmates reunite after a funeral and the street that Kevin Kline and William Hurt wander down after an early morning run in *The Big Chill*; the National Cemetery where "The Great Santini," portrayed by Robert Duvall, was buried in *The Great Santini*; and the bridge that Nick Nolte drives across as he sets off into the sunset in *The Prince of Tides*. The tour also showcases homes where the stars stayed while they were filming in town.

1006 Bay St., Beaufort, 843-838-2746
beaufforttoursllc.com

TIP

Beaufort Tours also offers walking, golf cart and step-on bus tours featuring history, the Civil War, Pat Conroy, Parris Island, and Gullah history.

OTHER *FORREST GUMP* FILMING LOCATIONS TO EXPLORE ON YOUR OWN

Four Square Gospel Church

The church where Forrest went to pray for shrimp.

Stoney Creek Presbyterian Chapel
155 County Rd. S-25-286, Yemassee

The Gump House

Where Forrest Gump and his mother, portrayed by Sally Field, lived when he was a child. The house is no longer standing, but the familiar entrance and long driveway from the "Run, Forrest, Run" scene are still visible.

The Bluff Plantation
3547 Combahee Rd., Yemassee

Greenbow Elementary

Where Sally Field met with the principal to discuss Forrest's intelligence testing scores.

Colleton Civic Center
494 Hampton St., Walterboro

Bubba Gump's House

Where Forrest went to visit Bubba's mother after his death.
145 Alston Rd., Beaufort

Gay Fish Company

They supplied all the shrimp for the film, and their dock is where Forrest paints "Jenny" on his boat.

1948 Sea Island Pkwy., St. Helena Island

Hunting Island State Park

Where the Vietnam battle scenes were filmed.

2555 Sea Island Pkwy., Hunting Island

ENJOY DINNER AND A MOVIE
AT PARK PLAZA CINEMA

Dinner and a movie make for the perfect date night, girls' night out, or family outing, and Park Plaza Cinema is the ideal location for them all. The independently owned boutique theater showcases mainstream current releases, as well as niche arthouse films, in five screening rooms, all with luxury reclining seats and swing arm tables. The lobby is more like a friend's living room, complete with sofas and chairs, dining tables, and even a bar to enjoy pre-movie food and beverages. The beverage menu is extensive, with wines by the glass or bottle, domestic and premium beers on draft or in cans, and even a selection of canned cocktails. The food menu goes well beyond your standard popcorn and candy, with classic pizzas, burgers, wraps, quesadillas, hot dogs, a charcuterie board, and a creative selection of flatbreads. The theater really feels like home, with the owners' dogs roaming the place—you can even bring your own (well-behaved) dog.

33 Office Park Rd., Ste. 201, Hilton Head Island, 843-715-0479
mannsparkplazacinema.com

TIP

Small dogs under 20 pounds are welcome. They must remain either in a carrier, on a leash on the floor, or on the owner's lap at all times (bring a blankie). Pets are not allowed on furniture.

35

GET YOUR GROOVE ON WITH STREET MUSIC

ON PARIS AVENUE

The slogan for the town of Port Royal is "Cool. Coastal. Far from Ordinary." It's the perfect definition for the town's Street Music on Paris Avenue series, which runs every spring and late summer. Part concert, part tailgate, the series brings national touring acts in all genres of music to Port Royal's main drag, Paris Avenue, for a good old-fashioned street party. Jamming for four weeks each spring (May and June) and late summer (August and September), residents of Port Royal and Beaufort and visitors strut their stuff, kick up their heels, shake a leg, and boogie down to live music from country to pop and blues to zydeco. Folks are encouraged to bring coolers of their favorite beverages, dinner, chairs, and of course, their dancing shoes.

Paris Avenue, between 9th and 10th Sts., 843-986-2200
portroyal.org

TIP

Before heading down Paris Avenue to the street party, make a pit stop at the Port Royal Cypress Wetlands and Rookery (friendsofportroyalcypresswetlands.org) for the sights and sounds of hundreds of egrets, herons, wood storks, alligators, and more.

BE ENTERTAINED
AT LOWCOUNTRY CELEBRATION PARK

Home to dozens of entertainment offerings, varied events, and much more, Lowcountry Celebration Park provides something for everyone throughout the year. Located between the Circle Center shopping center and the beach parking lot at the end of Pope Avenue, the park is just under 10 acres and includes a large lawn that overlooks the Performance Pavilion, a popular destination playground, walking trails and boardwalks, exercise stations, and restrooms. The Hilton Head Island Recreation Association manages park rentals and helps hold some of Hilton Head Island's biggest events at Lowcountry Celebration Park, including Hilton Head Wingfest, Jeep Island, Party in the Park + Maker's Fair, and much more. Other groups hold popular events there as well, including Sea Turtle Patrol Turtle Talks, Symphony Under the Stars, Crescendo, Hilton Head Island Jam, Latinos Unidos Food Festival, and the Fish and Grits Music Festival.

94 Pope Ave., Hilton Head Island, 843-681-7273
islandreccenter.org

LISTEN TO LIVE MUSIC ON THE WATER

AT PRESSLEY'S AT THE MARINA

Situated on Big Bay Creek at the Marina at Edisto Beach, Pressley's at the Marina features a laid-back, welcoming vibe, with varied seating options inside the colorful dining room and outside overlooking the water. Of course, the live music schedule come summer remains a huge hit with locals and visitors alike, but the year-round dining scene is what keeps Pressley's fans returning even when there isn't music on the menu that night. Open Thursday to Monday, bar service starts at 4 p.m. and dinner service starts 30 minutes later. There are lots of appetizers, including many seafood starters, several soups and salads (like their tasty she crab soup), and seafood-focused entrees that run the gamut (the local Edisto shrimp and the parmesan-encrusted grouper are rightfully popular), plus "off-island" choices like their "big a$$" ribeye. Given this combination, Pressley's remains a great place to eat, drink, and be very merry on Edisto Island.

3702 Docksite Rd., Edisto Beach, 843-869-9226
pressleysatthemarina.com

TIP

It's first-come, first-served at Pressley's, but veterans know the wait list for dining room seating starts at 4 p.m. sharp.

RUB ELBOWS WITH THE STARS

AT THE BEAUFORT INTERNATIONAL FILM FESTIVAL

For six days each February, Beaufort transforms into "Hollywood South," as the Beaufort International Film Festival (BIFF) brings in hundreds of filmmakers, cinematographers, screenwriters, and other industry professionals to celebrate the silver screen. Known as the "Film Capital of the South" in the 1980s and 1990s, Beaufort was the setting for dozens of films, including *The Big Chill*, *The Prince of Tides*, and *Forrest Gump*. When South Carolina's film industry waned in the early 2000s, avid local film buffs Ron and Rebecca Tucker created the Beaufort Film Society and launched the festival hoping to win some of those productions back—and let locals and tourists alike mingle with some of the biggest names in film. BIFF features dozens of shorts, documentaries, student films, and full-length films running from morning to night, along with workshops, receptions, and award ceremonies, and brings a touch of Hollywood to the Lowcountry.

843-522-3196
beaufortfilmfestival.com

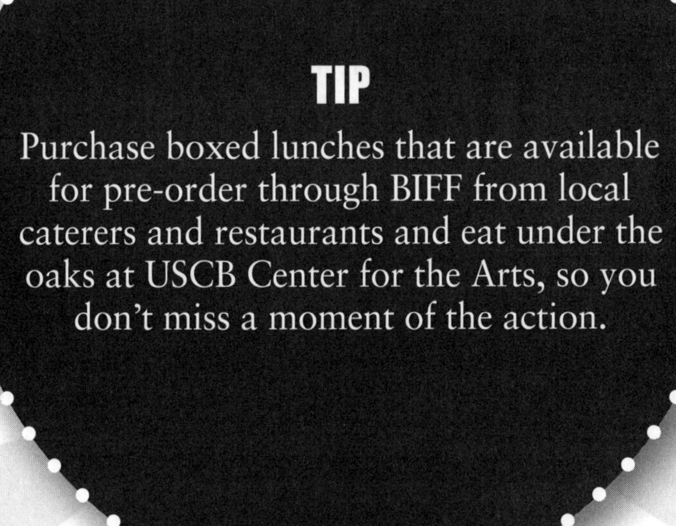

TIP

Purchase boxed lunches that are available for pre-order through BIFF from local caterers and restaurants and eat under the oaks at USCB Center for the Arts, so you don't miss a moment of the action.

MAKE MUSIC
AT THE KAZOOBIE KAZOO MUSEUM & FACTORY

Beaufort is home to one of the world's largest manufacturers of kazoos, the plastic musical instrument that utilizes a player's voice to create a musical sound. And what better way to get your kazoo on than exploring their 6,500-square-foot factory, where they build more than one million kazoos a year, along with other musical accessories. Daily guided factory tours include a short video presentation that highlights kazoo history; time to explore the Kazoo Museum; a demonstration of varied kazoos, including a wazoo, a kazoogle, a wazoogle, a kazobo, and an electric kazoo (who knew?); and a walk through the kazoo factory, with explanations on how they are made from start to finish. Guests even get to make their own kazoo to take home at the end of the tour, as well as endless shopping for musical treats at the gift shop.

12 John Galt Rd., Beaufort, 843-982-6387
thekazoofactory.com

GET YOUR FILL OF LIVE MUSIC, GRUB, AND VIEWS

AT THE FILLIN' STATION

There may not be a better setting in the Lowcountry for live music than the back deck at The Fillin' Station Waterfront Bar & Grill in Beaufort. With a busy line-up of live shows across many genres, but leaning toward rock and roll, the place locals call a "five-star dive bar" has long been known for its live music. But, there's so much more to "The Station" experience, including its great food and special "nights," a lively vibe inside and out on the deck overlooking Factory Creek, and friendly people (both staff and customers). Available to enjoy inside and out, the extensive menu includes classic and creative appetizers (like Wisconsin cheese curds, Angus steak bites, and duck bacon wontons); half-pound black Angus burgers and hot dogs; sandwiches (including their pickle juice-marinated chicken sandwich and po boys); seafood baskets; and tacos. The ever-changing Sunday brunch is a bargain, as are their special nights, including burgers, pork chops, shrimp, and more.

57 Sea Island Pkwy., Beaufort, 843-522-0230
facebook.com/thefillinstation

Biking on Hilton Head Island
Courtesy of Hilton Head Island-Bluffton VCB

SPORTS AND RECREATION

SPEND THE DAY AT THE BEACH
AT HUNTING ISLAND STATE PARK

Just 15 miles east of Beaufort's downtown waterfront sits Hunting Island State Park, 5,000 acres of postcard-perfect Lowcountry landscape—with miles of unspoiled beaches, meandering waterways, salt marsh grasses, and coastal wildlife. Add a 130-foot iconic lighthouse and you have a perfect Lowcountry outing. From frolicking in the surf, to sunbathing, building sandcastles, hiking miles of coastline or inland trails through lagoons and maritime forests, climbing to the top of the lighthouse for breathtaking views of the Atlantic Ocean, or exploring the nature center, Hunting Island State Park is the perfect playground for kids and kids at heart. There's also the unique option to book a tour to pristine St. Phillips Island, the former private retreat and vacation home of media mogul Ted Turner. Interpretive tours and unspoiled beaches await, with rentals of Turner's former house available for groups.

2555 Sea Island Pkwy., Hunting Island, 843-838-2011
southcarolinaparks.com/hunting-island

PICK UP BEACH EATS

Stop for breakfast or lunch—or better yet, pick up a picnic—on the way out to Hunting Island with these three can't-miss joints along the way.

Beedos Burgers

Specializing in popular breakfast sandwiches (aka "brekkies") and biscuits for breakfast, tasty smashburgers and sandwiches (aka "sandos") for lunch, plus old-fashioned soft serve ice cream, shakes, and malts for après-beach.

1634 Sea Island Pkwy., St. Helena Island, 843-612-2901
beedosburgers.com

Shrimp Shack

Serving up fried seafood sandwiches, baskets, and dinners since 1978.

1929 Sea Island Pkwy., St. Helena Island, 843-838-2962
facebook.com/shrimpshacksc

Johnson Creek Tavern

Boiled shrimp, steamed oysters, fried fish, and even Lowcountry boils, all served up with a beautiful marsh view.

2141 Sea Island Pkwy., St. Helena Island, 843-838-4166
johnsoncreektavern.com

GET OUTSIDE
WITH COASTAL EXPEDITIONS

With so much of the Lowcountry surrounded by salt marshes, winding waterways, and sandy beaches, there is no better way to explore the area than by water. Coastal Expeditions offers multiple ways to experience the nature, history, and ecology of the region by boat, kayak, and stand-up paddleboard. Let licensed captains do the driving on an eco-tour around Beaufort, St. Helena Island, Hunting Island, or St. Phillips Island, choosing from sunrise, sunset, dolphin, or private charter options. Those who prefer to do the driving and get their hands wet can rent a single or double kayak or paddleboard and create their own adventures within the estuaries around Hunting Island. Or go for a combination on a sunrise or sunset kayak or paddleboard tour along the rice fields and blackwater creeks of the ACE Basin. There is even a kayak safari tour that is perfect for young adventurers.

1928 Sea Island Pkwy., St. Helena Island, 843-929-2047
coastalexbeaufort.com

WATCH GOLF GREATS
AT THE RBC HERITAGE GOLF TOURNAMENT

Long known for its golf courses and golf resorts, Hilton Head Island also boasts one of the top PGA tournaments of the year. The RBC Heritage was founded in 1969, when Sea Pines visionary Charles Fraser partnered with Jack Nicklaus to create Harbour Town Golf Links specifically as a new stop on the PGA tour. Golf icon Arnold Palmer won that inaugural tournament, and the RBC Heritage has since grown into a highly coveted event on the tournament schedule. Played the week after the Masters, the RBC Heritage draws some of the top names in the sport and welcomes more than 100,000 spectators from across the country and around the globe. Tournament week features a traditional pipe and drum parade and cannon shot opening ceremonies, practice rounds, youth activities, merchandise tents, local and sponsored food and beverage concession stands, lounges and clubs, and some of the top golf action in the world.

11 Lighthouse Ln., Hilton Head Island, 843-671-2448
rbcheritage.com

TIP

Parking and traffic during the RBC Heritage are challenges. But bicycle parking is complimentary, and all bike paths throughout Hilton Head Island lead to The Sea Pines Resort.

SLEEP AT THE BEACH
AT EDISTO BEACH STATE PARK

One of four oceanfront state parks in the state, Edisto Beach State Park features two distinct park areas—one oceanside and one marsh side—both offering unique experiences. Tent and RV camping are available on both sides, with many sites being steps from beach access to the Atlantic Ocean or in the shaded maritime forest. The park also offers seven furnished cabins that were built by the Civilian Conservation Corps in the 1930s. Hiking and biking abound in the park, with more than four miles of ADA-accessible trails that lead to hammock islands, as well as a Spanish mount—an ancient shell midden created by Edisto Indigenous peoples dating back to 2000 BC—along with 1.5 miles of oceanfront hiking. The park also features an Environmental Learning Center housing a collection of fossils, interactive displays, and live animals to help illustrate the importance of the ACE Basin estuarine reserve and its impact on the Lowcountry.

8377 State Cabin Rd., Edisto Island, 843-869-2156
southcarolinaparks.com/edisto-beach

GET ON TWO WHEELS
WITH WHEELZ HILTON HEAD

Long known as a biking-friendly Lowcountry destination, Hilton Head Island is a gold level bicycle friendly community that features more than 60 miles of varied public bike paths and nature trails. Traveling by two wheels is a great way to get around anywhere on the island, including on the beach (which sometimes depends on the tides, the wind, and other weather). Open since 2019 and conveniently located on a bike path less than a mile from Coligny Beach Park, the vast Wheelz Hilton Head operation features a large inventory of high-quality rental cycling equipment and golf carts, plus a wide array of retail merchandise and more. Their helpful staff will find the appropriate rental for each person, with options for half-day to one-month rentals including single-speed cruisers in sizes for the entire family; step-through bikes; adult trikes; and lots of attachments, including child trailers, child seats, child trailer cycles, flatbed cargo trailers, and varied pet carriers.

1 Executive Park Rd., Ste. A, Hilton Head Island, 843-842-4445
rentwheelz.com

TIP

Wheelz Hilton Head will even deliver bike rentals that are for three days or longer.

46

NURTURE NATURE
AT PINCKNEY ISLAND NATIONAL WILDLIFE REFUGE

This 4,000-plus-acre refuge includes Pinckney Island, along with several smaller islands and hammocks that were donated to the federal government in 1975 for the sole purpose of preserving the wildlife resources. Originally the home of Indigenous peoples during the Archaic Period and then the plantation home of Revolutionary War general and signer of the US Constitution, Charles Cotesworth Pinckney, Pinckney Island was generally abandoned after the Civil War. Converted to a hunting preserve in the late 1930s, trees were replanted, ponds were built to attract waterfowl, and 70 percent of the farm fields were placed back into cultivation. Managed today by the US Fish and Wildlife Service, the island is filled with natural wildlife and scenery and offers over 14 miles of trails for hiking, biking, bird watching, and photography, along with explanatory signage on Lowcountry birds, butterflies, grasses, and animals found throughout the refuge.

Hwy. 278, Bluffton, 843-784-2468
fws.gov/refuge/pinckney-island

47

ENJOY DISC GOLF AND THE WATER

AT SERGEANT JASPER PARK

Conveniently situated just off busy I-95 and north of Hardeeville proper, 321-acre Sergeant Jasper Park is a world away. The popular park features nine stocked fishing lakes; five short walking trails (all one mile or less); the pristine 130-acre Forest Preserve; birdwatching; a canoe/kayak launch area, as well as canoe and kayak rentals; many events (including a popular 5K run); their banquet hall/picnic shelter; the helpful office/activity center; and the Sarge Disc Golf Course. This popular 20-hole course is fun for both experts and first-timers. Those looking for further boating and fishing possibilities in Jasper County will find more than a half-dozen other boat landings in the county, including several with docks and three that provide access to the meandering Savannah River.

1458 Red Dam Rd., Hardeeville, 843-784-5130
jaspercountysc.gov

TIP

Along with heading to Hardeeville's Sergeant Jasper Park, disc golf fans will want to head to UDisc (udisc.com) to find other disc golf locations in the Lowcountry, including Hover Links at First Presbyterian Church and Hilton Head Island Recreation's "Rec Graveyard," both on Hilton Head Island.

EXPLORE A LOWCOUNTRY PARADISE
AT MONTAGE PALMETTO BLUFF

Southern hospitality meets dreamy decadence amongst 20,000 acres of wilderness, wildlife, salt marshes, and more along the May River in Bluffton at Montage Palmetto Bluff. With a dedication to conservation over development, the property is a playground for the naturalist and sportsman alike. From golf to fitness and wellness, fishing and sporting clays to hiking and biking, racquet sports to boating, and canoeing or kayaking over 32 miles of coastline, the outdoors awaits. Visitors can also get in touch with their inner artists by taking a class at Flow Gallery + Workshop or getting their hands dirty while picking up some gardening tips at Palmetto Bluff Farm. There's also dining at a variety of village venues featuring Lowcountry specialties and grab and go options or several resort offerings from casual to fine dining, as well as a modern speakeasy. For added decadence, stay the night in luxe accommodations that feature sumptuous Southern decor, opulent bathrooms, and private verandas.

477 Mount Pelia Rd., Bluffton, 843-706-6500
montage.com/palmettobluff

GET ADVENTUROUS
WITH OUTSIDE HILTON HEAD

What started as a windsurfing school in 1979 has expanded into a full-service outdoor outfitter offering dozens of activities and programs. There's a wide choice of dolphin tours, beachcombing cruises, Daufuskie Island tours, and sunset and fireworks cruises on both power boats and sailboats. Hunt for shark teeth, rent a pontoon boat, charter a fishing boat, go shark fishing, or try your hand at tubing or water skiing. For the more adventurous, rent a kayak or stand-up paddleboard or take a lesson, go on a full moon kayak tour, try kayak fishing, or participate in a surf camp. For landlubbers, they offer e-bike tours and rentals to explore the miles of bike paths throughout Hilton Head Island. Or let them create a personalized private tour combining any of their activities. No matter what kind of Lowcountry adventure is on the bucket list, Outside Hilton Head can make it happen.

50 Shelter Cove Ln., Hilton Head Island, 843-686-6996
outsidehiltonhead.com

TIP

Tours fill up early and quickly, especially in the summer months. Make a reservation as soon as you know the program and dates you are interested in. Reservations are accepted up to 12 months in advance.

50

GO WILD
IN WALTERBORO

Just a few miles off I-95, visitors will experience Lowcountry history, culture, recreation, and education at the Walterboro Wildlife Center and the Walterboro Wildlife Sanctuary. Visitors start at the Wildlife Center for an introduction to the outdoor wonderland, with interpretive exhibits explaining the importance of Lowcountry swamps and native habitats. Then, they head to the Sanctuary, a 600-acre park, which is part of the 350,000-acre ACE Basin, made up by the Ashepoo, Combahee, and Edisto Rivers. The sanctuary features a "braided creek" swamp—a tangled network of creeks that diverge and reunite, resembling a braid. Hike or bike on boardwalks, bridges, and more than four miles of trails—including segments of the old Charleston-to-Savannah stagecoach route. Be on the lookout for Lowcountry flora and fauna like Spanish moss-draped live oaks, cypress knees, wildflowers, wild turkey, deer, beaver, alligators, birds, and more.

100 S Jefferies Blvd., Walterboro, 843-782-6081
visitwalterborosc.org

Parking and access for the Walterboro Wildlife Sanctuary
Corner of S Jeffries Blvd. and Washington St.
At the end of Detreville St.
At the corner of S Jeffries Blvd. and Ivanhoe Rd.

51

SLITHER OVER
TO EDISTO ISLAND SERPENTARIUM

Although you might think dragons and sea serpents, the Edisto Island Serpentarium is a one-of-a-kind collection of all things reptiles. With a mission statement of "the recognition, preservation, and study of the world of reptiles," this museum-cum-wildlife park features hundreds of slithering snakes in natural pits, climbing trees, hanging from branches like Spanish moss, and frolicking in landscaped ponds. There are tropical snakes, venomous snakes native to the region, and venomous and non-venomous snakes from around the world, along with four alligator ponds with more than 40 alligators—ranging in age from juvenile to adult. Two crocodile enclosures, several varieties of lizards from around the world, multiple species of native American turtles, and various land tortoise species from around the globe—including an African Spur-Thigh tortoise, the third-largest land turtle in the world—complete the prehistoric scene, along with daily educational talks and feeding opportunities.

1374 Hwy. 174, Edisto Island, 843-869-1171
edistoserpentarium.com

GET HEALTHIER

AT HILTON HEAD HEALTH WELLNESS RESORT & SPA

Founded in 1976, Hilton Head Health Wellness Resort & Spa (aka H3) has evolved into a world-class all-inclusive wellness resort offering a wide variety of packages. Fitness is a big part of any wellness resort, and H3 doesn't disappoint, thanks to lots of healthy offerings focusing on cardio, strength, stretch/recovery, walking, and more. These daily offerings take place in H3's state-of-the-art facilities, including a heated pool, along with many educational lectures, and participants have a choice of more than two dozen activities every day. One can enjoy a packed wellness schedule or a more relaxed approach, including appointments at H3's Indigo Spa (which is open to the public). H3's nutritious food is so much more than three daily and tasty meals at True restaurant. There are also Fit Bites snacks, chef demos, Chef's Table dinners, and nutrition-focused lectures. Participants can stay at H3's stunning 30-room Sweetgrass Inn on the H3 campus or elsewhere (typically at a nearby villa).

14 Valencia Rd., Hilton Head Island, 843-785-7292
hhhealth.com

STAY IN A CCC-BUILT CABIN

ON THE EDISTO RIVER

One of 16 South Carolina state parks built by the Civilian Conservation Corps (CCC) between 1933 and 1942, Givhans Ferry State Park (24 miles northeast of Walterboro) is a 988-acre park situated at the end of a 23-mile section of the Edisto River that begins at Colleton State Park, and it is part of the 62-mile Edisto River Canoe and Kayak Trail. The park offers stays in historic two-bedroom fully equipped CCC-built cabins overlooking the river; varied camping; full-service tubing trips with Edisto River Adventures (edistoriveradventures.com); kayak and canoe put-in; the River House, with a camp store and a riverfront back porch; and the 1.5-mile River Bluff Nature Trail overlooking limestone bluffs. Other CCC-built state park cabins can be found in the Lowcountry at Edisto Beach State Park, as well as at seven other state parks across South Carolina.

746 Givhans Ferry Rd., Ridgeville, 843-873-0692
southcarolinaparks.com/givhans-ferry

TIP

St. George-based Carolina Heritage Outfitters (canoesc.com) offers another unique way to paddle and stay on the Edisto River, thanks to their rustic and secluded treehouses, plus day trips and more.

GET ON THE WATER

WITH EDISTO WATERSPORTS & TACKLE

Owned by Captain Dillard Young and his wife, Master Naturalist Lindsey Young, Edisto Watersports & Tackle provides one-stop shopping for getting on the water around Edisto Island. They offer a variety of fishing charters, including three- and four-hour inshore/near shore options and five- and seven-hour offshore trips. Depending on the trip and season, a wide variety of fish may be caught, and the crew will clean and filet them to be enjoyed later. In addition, their 90-minute ACE Basin dolphin/history river boat tours and one-hour sunset boat trips provide a great way to explore the nature and history of Edisto Island from out on the water. They also feature two-hour guided kayak tours, plus full moon and sunrise offerings, as well as rental kayaks and paddle boards. Plus, adjacent sister business Edisto Bike Rentals offers bike and golf cart rentals to use while on land.

3731 Docksite Rd., Edisto Island, 843-869-0663
edistowatersports.net

TAKE A TRIP
TO FAMED FRIPP ISLAND

What could be better than a beach getaway to famed Fripp Island in South Carolina's Lowcountry? With more than three miles of pristine beaches (including lots of easy beach access), loads of Lowcountry waterways and marshes, two golf courses, tennis courts, pickleball, and an impressive activity and nature center, there is truly something for everyone on family- and pet-friendly Fripp Island. There are mary varied accommodation options through Fripp Island Golf & Beach Resort, including unique waterfront homes, condos, and more. They also have varied vacation gear for rent, including electric golf carts, kayaks, fishing gear, boats, and bicycles. There are family-oriented programming opportunities all year, from Camp Fripp in the summer to golf cart scavenger hunts, trivia, and more. That activity will work up an appetite, and Fripp Island accommodates hungry visitors with varied restaurants and watering holes across the island.

201 Tarpon Blvd., Fripp Island, 843-838-1558
frippislandresort.com

TIP

There's no better place to devour one of Pat Conroy's books than Fripp Island. He lived on the island for many years, and no one describes the sights, smells, and sounds of the Lowcountry better than Conroy.

56

EXPLORE LOWCOUNTRY WILD WONDERS
AT DONNELLEY WILDLIFE MANAGEMENT AREA

At 8,047 sprawling acres, Donnelley Wildlife Management Area is truly a cross-section of the Lowcountry's wild wonders and encompasses a wide diversity of wetland and upland habitats, featuring forested wetlands, tidal marshes, rice fields, and agricultural lands, as well as several upland habitats, including a large stand of longleaf pine. Situated just off Charleston Highway (US 17), at Highway 303 near Green Pond, there's a designated walking trail (Boynton Nature Trail), plus miles of dirt roads for hikers and bikers to explore. There's also an 11-mile driving tour that's highly recommended. Wildlife watching opportunities include birdwatching (generally late winter to early spring) and abundant alligators in the managed wetlands, which are most often seen from late February through mid-November. This Lowcountry gem is operated by the South Carolina Department of Natural Resources. Visit their website in advance to make sure the area is not closed due to scheduled hunts.

585 Donnelley Dr., Green Pond, 843-844-8957
dnr.sc.gov

GET OUT
ON THE SPANISH MOSS TRAIL

The popular Spanish Moss Trail is a part of a still-growing rails-to-trails greenway located in Beaufort County. Following the former Magnolia Rail Line, it has become a must-experience Lowcountry outdoor activity for more than 100,000 residents and visitors each year. Currently, the trail is a 10-mile, 12-foot-wide, paved path dedicated to those who walk, run, bike, or fish—offering spectacular Lowcountry water and marsh vistas, coastal marine and wildlife viewing, and historic points of interest (with informative markers) as it meanders through Spanish moss-draped neighborhoods and beautiful wetlands. It also provides easy access to the dining, shopping, accommodations, and public spaces of historic downtown areas in and around Beaufort and Port Royal. The trail will eventually run at least 16 miles. It's a featured and favorite trail of the Rails to Trails Conservancy for good reason.

spanishmosstrail.com

58

PLAN A HILTON HEAD ISLAND GETAWAY
TO THE SEA PINES RESORT

A getaway to The Sea Pines Resort, a gated community on Hilton Head Island, is a special Lowcountry island adventure unlike any other. A resort experience starts with a great place to stay, and Sea Pines accommodates with varied villas, spacious homes, plus the elegant setting of the Inn & Club at Harbour Town. Of course, The Sea Pines Resort is well-known for its world-class golf, including Pete Dye-designed Harbour Town Golf Links, Heron Point by Pete Dye, and Atlantic Dunes by Davis Love III. Other Sea Pines recreational possibilities include climbing the iconic red-and-white striped Harbour Town lighthouse; an extensive tennis facility (including packages, instruction, and more); pickleball; biking on 15 miles of trails; horseback riding; a full fitness center; miles of beaches and a beach club; varied watersports; lots of shopping at the upscale Shops at Sea Pines Center and in Harbour Town; and delicious coastal dining.

32 Greenwood Dr., Hilton Head Island
866-561-8802 or 843-785-3333
seapines.com

SEA PINES DINING

Diverse dining possibilities in Sea Pines include seafood, an oyster bar, and 270-degree views at Quarterdeck under the famed red-and-white Harbour Town Lighthouse; Links, overlooking Harbour Town Golf Links; oceanfront Coast at Sea Pines Beach Club; Southern barbecue and more at Fraser's Tavern; outdoor dining at Harbourside; the prerequisite Sea Pines dining experience at the Salty Dog Cafe, with a great vibe, grub, and views; a Lowcountry Produce outpost; a tasty start to a Sea Pines morning at Harbour Town Bakery & Café; and market fare at Quarterdeck Market and Surfside Market.

59

EXPERIENCE PRIMITIVE LOWCOUNTRY COASTLINE LIFE

AT BOTANY BAY

Unlike any other destination or attraction in the Lowcountry, Botany Bay Heritage Preserve and Wildlife Management Area features 3,363 pristine acres on the remote northeast corner of Edisto Island adjacent to the Atlantic Ocean, near the North Edisto River. Managed by South Carolina's Department of Natural Resources, the preserved features of undeveloped Botany Bay include maritime forest, tidal marshes, managed wetlands, coastal scrub/shrub areas, and the wheelchair-accessible causeway that leads to "boneyard" beach (accessible at low tide), with its massive downed driftwood trees, considered Botany Bay's highlight by many. Inland, historic shell rings, several outbuildings from Edisto Island's historic Bleak Hall Plantation, and artifacts from the Alexander Bache US Coast Survey Line are also worth exploring. The three-mile driving (or hiking or biking) tour also features many points of historic and natural interest.

Botany Bay Rd., Edisto Island, 843-844-8957
dnr.sc.gov

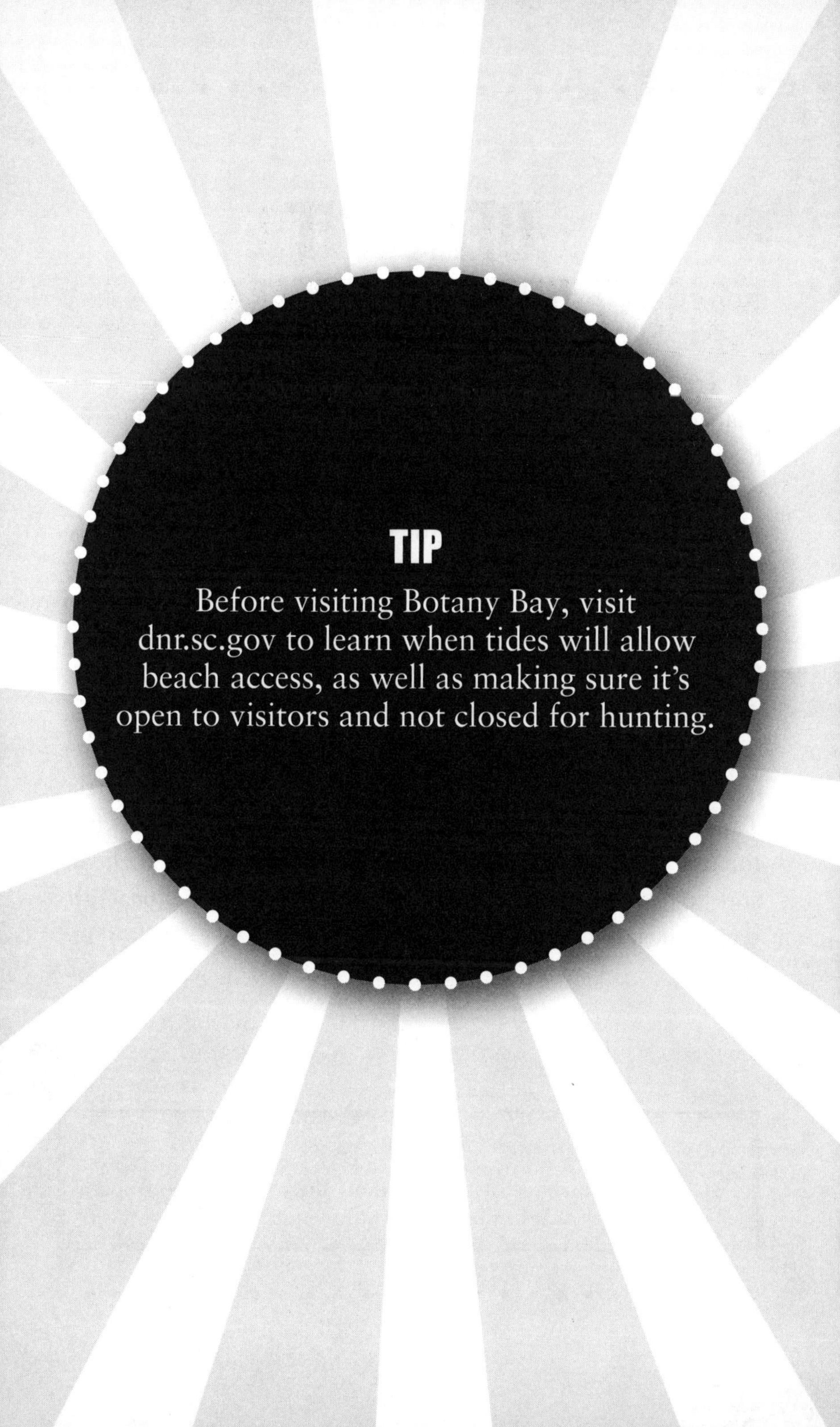

TIP

Before visiting Botany Bay, visit dnr.sc.gov to learn when tides will allow beach access, as well as making sure it's open to visitors and not closed for hunting.

60

BEACH IT
ON HILTON HEAD ISLAND

Of course, other parts of the Lowcountry feature great beaches, but Hilton Head Island is rightfully world-famous for its wide stretches of sandy strand ideal for beaching it, as well as walking and biking. Heading from South Beach in Sea Pines to the northeast along the beach, there are many named beaches and beach access points. Beach markers are posted at the dune line starting at South Beach and go northeast to BM #134 at Port Royal's Fish Haul Creek. If the marker includes a letter after the number, it is designating beach access (like BM 59A at the Coligny Beach access). There's metered parking at many beach access points, and both cash and credit cards are accepted. Those with disabilities can take advantage of the Town of Hilton Head Island's great "Wheelchair Program" for use at Coligny Beach Park and Islanders Beach Park. Be sure to look for "Sharing Shack" stations along the beach to recycle beach items.

hiltonheadislandsc.gov

TIP

Beachcombers and cyclists should know there's a tidal pool south of Burkes Beach that can be crossed at low tide.

HILTON HEAD ISLAND PUBLIC BEACH ACCESS

Fish Haul Beach Park
120 Mitchelville Rd.

Historic Mitchelville Freedom Park
226 Beach City Rd.

Islanders Beach Park
94 Folly Field Rd.

Folly Field Beach Park
55 Starfish Dr.

Driessen Beach Park
64 Bradley Beach Rd.

Burkes Beach
60 Burkes Beach Rd.

Coligny Beach Park
1 Coligny Cir.

Alder Lane Beach
2 Woodward Ave.

South Beach
(in Sea Pines, a gated community), Black Duck Pl.

Gullah culture
Courtesy of Lowcountry Tourism Commission

CULTURE AND HISTORY

61

GET THE LOWDOWN ON THE LOWCOUNTRY
AT A VISITORS CENTER

Visitors centers across the country are great places to talk to experts about the area, and that's especially true in the Lowcountry, thanks to four unique and well-situated options. Conveniently located just off I-95, historic Frampton Plantation House and Lowcountry Visitors Center provides a one-stop resource for all of the Lowcountry, as well as a large gift shop that features Lowcountry books, art, foodstuffs, and more. Situated in downtown Beaufort in the historic Arsenal building and also including a great gift shop, the helpful Beaufort Visitor Center represents Beaufort, Port Royal, and the neighboring Sea Islands, including Lady's Island, St. Helena Island, Hunting Island, and Fripp Island. Finally, Bluffton, Hilton Head Island, and Daufuskie Island visitors have two possible stops, with one in downtown Bluffton and the other in the middle of Hilton Head Island. Each of these three Lowcountry tourism organizations also feature comprehensive websites.

VISITORS CENTERS

Frampton Plantation House and Lowcountry Visitors Center

1 Low Country Ln., Yemassee
800-528-6870 or 843-717-3090
southcarolinalowcountry.com

Beaufort Visitor Center

713 Craven St., Beaufort
843-525-8500
beaufortsc.org

Hilton Head Island-Bluffton Chamber of Commerce and Visitor & Convention Bureau

1 Chamber of Commerce Dr., Ste. A, Hilton Head Island
843-785-3673

216 Bluffton Rd., Bluffton
843-757-3673
hiltonheadisland.org

62

GET TO KNOW THE PRINCE OF SCRIBES
AT THE PAT CONROY LITERARY CENTER

Part library, part museum, the Pat Conroy Literary Center was created a year after its namesake's premature passing to honor and showcase the life and writings of the beloved Southern writer for future generations. This literary treasure trove is filled with memorabilia from Conroy's Lowcountry years in high school; photos from his time at The Citadel and his year of teaching on Daufuskie Island; handwritten pages from several of his novels; his writing desk; the storied flight jacket of his father, the real "Great Santini"; and keepsakes from the local filming of adaptations of his bestsellers, including *The Great Santini* and *The Prince of Tides*. The center also pays homage to this literary legend by hosting readings by acclaimed regional and national authors; offering writing classes; sponsoring lectures, master classes, and other special events; hosting literary arts education programs in collaboration with schools; and holding the annual Pat Conroy Literary Festival in the fall.

601 Bladen St., Beaufort, 843-379-7025
patconroyliterarycenter.org

TIP

Visit on Sundays and have the opportunity to tour the center with docent Kathy Conroy Harvey, Pat Conroy's sister.

63

PLUNGE INTO
LOWCOUNTRY MARINE HERITAGE

With a mission to preserve and conserve the environmental, cultural, and economic benefits of the Port Royal Sound surrounding the Lowcountry region from Hilton Head Island to Beaufort, the Port Royal Sound Foundation created the free-of-charge Maritime Center to educate and share the history, marine wildlife, and ecology of the area. Visitors can learn about the maritime history and culture of the Lowcountry area; see water-oriented artwork and artifacts from around Port Royal Sound; get up-close and personal with native wildlife, like alligators, snakes, turtles, and fish; learn about local seafood traditions; take guided nature hikes and naturalist-led kayak excursions; or simply enjoy the quiet beauty of the salt marshes from the docks overlooking the sound. Visitors might even spot a dolphin. Salty Dog Cruise hosts sunset cruises and special events on their 63-foot catamaran departing from the Port Royal Sound Foundation Maritime Center.

310 Okatie Hwy., Okatie, 843-645-7774
portroyalsoundfoundation.org

64

CELEBRATE GULLAH CULTURE
AT HISTORIC PENN CENTER

Beaufort is often considered the epicenter of the Lowcountry's Gullah community—descendants of Africans who were enslaved in the area. Penn School was created in 1862 on St. Helena Island by Northern abolitionists to serve as one of the nation's first schools for formerly enslaved people, with classes originally held at the 1855 Brick Baptist Church. In 1864, freedman Hastings Gantt donated land he owned at Penn's current location for a permanent education building. After the school closed in the late 1940s, Penn School became Penn Center, offering social services to the island's residents. Today, the expanded compound is part of the Reconstruction Era National Historical Park and serves as an educational mission for Gullah and Reconstruction history. The welcome center and museum are packed with displays of historic documents, oral histories, and handicrafts of the Reconstruction era. Guided and self-guided walking tours explore the site's 25 buildings, including Gantt Cottage, where Martin Luther King Jr. stayed during various civil rights interracial conferences.

16 Penn Center Cir. W, St. Helena Island, 843-838-7105
penncenter.com

OTHER GULLAH LANDMARKS NEARBY

St. Helena Parish Chapel of Ease

Just a mile down the road from Penn Center sit the remnants of the Chapel of Ease, built using tabby construction between 1742 and 1747 and standing as a symbol of Reconstruction.

17 Lands End Rd., St. Helena Island, 843-522-1712
sthelenas1712.org

St. Helena Memorial Gardens

The final resting site of many of St. Helena's Gullah community and notable South Carolina African Americans, as well as that of legendary Southern writer Pat Conroy.

Ernest Dr., St. Helena Island

Gullah Grub

Classic cuisine prepared following Gullah traditions, like gumbo, barbecue chicken, and fried fish and shrimp, served with seasonal side dishes.

877 Sea Island Pkwy., St. Helena Island, 843-838-3841
gullahgrub.com

65

UNCOVER THE WONDERS OF THE LOWCOUNTRY
AT THE COASTAL DISCOVERY MUSEUM

Set on 70 acres at historic Honey Horn, the Coastal Discovery Museum on Hilton Head Island is a Smithsonian affiliate that offers unique experiences, art exhibitions, tours, talks, workshops, and events. Visitors can explore nature trails, salt marsh boardwalks, a butterfly habitat, a dragonfly pond, a renowned camellia garden, and historic buildings surrounded by centuries-old live oaks draped in Spanish moss. There's something for all ages and groups, including interacting with lots of wildlife, such as baby alligators, horseshoe crabs, lizards, and more; creating indigo tie-dye keepsakes; or making a Gullah sweetgrass basket, all while learning about the history of this diverse region. It's also the home of their coastal-leaning and well-stocked Museum Store, the Farmers Market of Hilton Head, and the island's juried Art Market at Historic Honey Horn every April. Beyond the grounds, off-site adventures include birding on Pinckney Island and Gullah Heritage Trail Tours.

70 Honey Horn Dr., Hilton Head Island, 843-689-6767
coastaldiscovery.org

TIP

There is no admission charge (and parking is free), but donations are accepted to help keep this Lowcountry gem open for everyone to enjoy.

EXPLORE LOWCOUNTRY CULTURE AT THE COLLETON MUSEUM & FARMERS MARKET

Colleton County is considered the "Front Porch of the Lowcountry," due to its location and proximity to I-95. Since 1985, the Colleton Museum & Farmers Market in Walterboro has strived to preserve and promote the historical, natural, cultural, and agricultural heritage of the county. Through exhibits of the Revolutionary and Civil Wars, the impact of the ACE Basin on the region, plantation life, Colleton life through the years, and a re-creation of Varn's General Store, Colleton County's history has been preserved and interpreted for locals and visitors alike. Rotating cultural and historical exhibits and artistic workshops and classes throughout the year focus on the region, along with a farmers market on Saturdays and Tuesdays from May to December, offering local vegetables and fruit, farm fresh eggs, honey, handmade crafts, art, baked goods, and prepared foods. There's even a commercial kitchen incubator.

506 E Washington St., Walterboro, 843-549-2303
colletonmuseum.org

67

HONOR AMERICA'S HISTORY

AT THE RECONSTRUCTION ERA NATIONAL HISTORICAL PARK

As the Beaufort area was captured by Civil War Union forces during the Battle of Port Royal, many White residents fled, leaving behind their property and enslaved people, which left more than 10,000 newly freed African Americans to help usher in the nation's Reconstruction Era. Created in 2017 as a National Monument (and redesignated a National Historical Park in 2019), this time period park, spread across four locations throughout the Beaufort area, commemorates this monumental turning point in our nation's history. The park includes downtown's Visitor Center and walking tours of prominent Civil War and Reconstruction buildings, locations, and memorials; Camp Saxton, which served as one of the first recruiting depots and training facilities for African American soldiers; Darrah Hall, the oldest building on the Penn Center campus; and the grounds of the 1855 Brick Baptist Church, where many of the early classes at Penn Center were held.

706 Craven St., Beaufort, 843-962-0039
nps.gov/reer

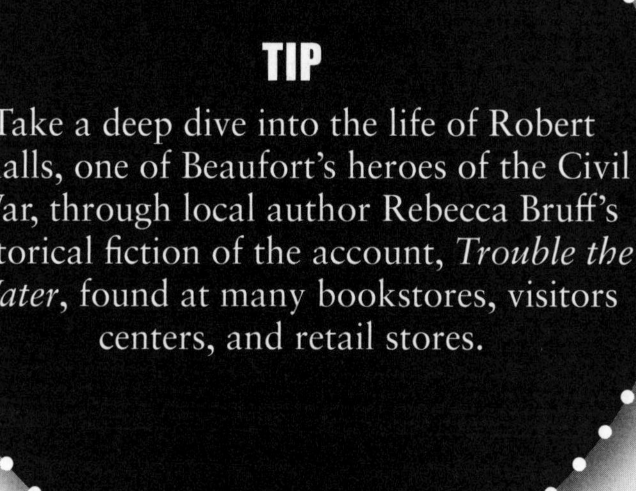

TIP

Take a deep dive into the life of Robert Smalls, one of Beaufort's heroes of the Civil War, through local author Rebecca Bruff's historical fiction of the account, *Trouble the Water*, found at many bookstores, visitors centers, and retail stores.

GET A FILL-UP OF LOCAL HISTORY

AT THE MORRIS CENTER FOR LOWCOUNTRY HERITAGE

Located in the heart of downtown Ridgeland in a former Sinclair Service Station, the Morris Center for Lowcountry Heritage preserves and interprets the history and culture of the region. Paying homage to its founder, local businessman and entrepreneur Danny Morris, and capturing the spirit of his beloved community, the center features permanent and rotating exhibits, like "The Battle of Honey Hill" and "Discover the American Revolution in South Carolina." It also hosts workshops and classes that reflect the region, including indigo dyeing, printmaking, glass mosaics, and sweetgrass basket weaving. The center also curates and presents educational programs from panel discussions to history talks to oral histories and conversations. From the historic venue to docent-led guided tours, rich self-guided exhibits, and special events like Story Fest, the center celebrates the region's rich heritage and the area's unique sense of place.

10782 S Jacob Smart Blvd., Ridgeland, 843-284-9227
morrisheritagecenter.org

TIP

Plan your visit around lunchtime and walk down the block to Fiddler's Seafood (fiddlersseafoodrestaurant.com) for a fried fish basket. Or pick up some tasty seafood around the corner at their seafood market.

69

PRAISE THE PAST
AT OLD SHELDON CHURCH RUINS

Originally known as Prince William's Parish Church, Old Sheldon Church in Yemassee was built between 1745 and 1753 in the Greek Revival style. Burned down by the British in 1779 during the Revolutionary War, it was rebuilt in 1826. Although it was generally believed to be burned again in 1865 as General William Tecumseh Sherman marched north, recently unearthed accounts say that it possibly wasn't burned, but simply ransacked. In either case, the ruins as they stand today, with their massive columns and floor-to-ceiling arched empty window openings, are a testament to the solid construction and master craftsmanship of the period. Set amongst the majestic oaks and Spanish moss of the Lowcountry and surrounded by solemn gravesites, including that of Colonel William Bull, who is credited with assisting General James Edward Oglethorpe with the original surveying and physical layout of Savannah's grid pattern of streets and squares, this magical spot is a haven for photographers, history buffs, and worshipers.

Old Sheldon Church Rd., Yemassee, 843-522-1712
sthelenas1712.org

SEE THE MAKING OF MARINES
AT PARRIS ISLAND

Home to one of two Marine Corps Recruit Depots in the country, Parris Island—south of Port Royal and five miles from downtown Beaufort—has been the training ground for tens of thousands of Marine recruits as they begin their career of service to our country since 1915. The 13-week training program is conducted amidst the homes and military buildings that were constructed on the property after the Great Sea Island Storm of 1893, when it was a naval station. Today, guests can visit Parris Island and learn about the history and importance of this stalwart training base. Visitors can explore the grounds as part of a "windshield tour," including seeing several monuments commemorating the history of the island, and visit the 10,000-square-foot Parris Island Museum, featuring thousands of artifacts, images, and other materials that illustrate the history of the Marines, Parris Island, and the entire Beaufort area. With advanced scheduling, visitors can also play golf at Legends Golf Course.

577 Blvd. de France, Parris Island, 843-228-3650
mcrdpi.marines.mil

TIP

Visitors need to show a valid driver's license and proof of automobile insurance to enter the gate. Be sure to have both ready before arrival.

71

LEARN ABOUT
THE LOWCOUNTRY'S RICH GULLAH CULTURE

Opened in 2025 to rave reviews, the Bluffton Gullah Cultural Heritage Center located at Ma Daisy's Porch is a great place to begin an exploration of Gullah history and culture in the Lowcountry. Conveniently perched right on historic May River Road in downtown Bluffton and through varied ever-changing exhibits, programs, events, dining, and an open-air market, this major attraction provides a world-class stand-alone destination to explore the Gullah community's distinctive sense of place. Chef B's is an epicurean hotspot where coastal culture and cuisine collide, and features a menu that celebrates the vibrant and rich essence of Gullah life and foodways. Also located on the property is Backus Bakery, a decadent pâtisserie featuring savory and sweet homemade baked goods. Be it stuffed beignets, extravagant cakes, or meat-filled French breads, their tasty creations celebrate cultural ingenuity.

1255 May River Rd., Bluffton, 561-352-8608
blufftongullah.org

72

ADMIRE ANTEBELLUM ARCHITECTURE
AT THE JOHN MARK VERDIER HOUSE

Built about 1804 by John Mark Verdier, this classic Federal-style home is the only historic planter's house in Beaufort that is open to the public, and it presents an accurate portrait of how Beaufort's elite lived during the antebellum period. Verdier was a successful local merchant in the lucrative indigo trade of the period. Building his house to represent his position in society, the grand home features a double front pedimented portico supported by Doric columns with views of the water; an archway in the central hall bolstered by Corinthian columns; mantles with elaborate cornices adorning the principle entertaining rooms—the parlor, dining room, and second floor ballroom; and authentic period furnishings, including several artifacts original to the home. It was spared by Sherman's march, as the house was turned into a Union Army headquarters, and a group of Beaufort visionaries rallied to save the historic house in 1944. After years of restoration, it opened as a museum in 1975.

801 Bay St., Beaufort, 843-379-6335
historicbeaufort.org

73

EXPLORE AMERICA'S FIRST SELF-GOVERNED TOWN OF FREEDMEN

At the height of the Civil War, many escaped and abandoned enslaved people, whose owners had fled, congregated on Hilton Head Island. These industrious people created their own town on the grounds of the former Drayton Plantation, with the assistance of Union General Ormsby Mitchel. They constructed streets, built homes, elected officials, enacted laws, paid taxes, and named their town Mitchelville. When the war ended, the property reverted back to the Drayton family, and its inhabitants moved on. Today, direct descendants of Mitchelville residents and others are preserving and restoring the community and its story of freedom as a work in progress called Historic Mitchelville Freedom Park. Featuring a covered gazebo, historical exhibits like the Praise House and an original bateau, "ghost" structures representing the original homes of the community, and kiosks telling the Mitchelville story through words and images, the self-guided park serves to educate, enlighten, and inspire the public about the sacrifice and perseverance of freedmen.

40 Harriet Tubman Way, Hilton Head Island, 843-255-7301
exploremitchelville.org

GET CARRIED AWAY BY A CARRIAGE TOUR
IN HISTORIC BEAUFORT

Taking a carriage tour of historic downtown Beaufort provides a genteel way to learn the history, see the sights, and get an overview of what to see and do while in town. Hearkening back to an earlier time when horses provided the main means of transportation throughout the Lowcountry and beyond, two companies offer popular carriage tours in Beaufort, which include knowledgeable narration and stops to view historic homes and other buildings, including movie locations (like *The Big Chill* and *The Great Santini*). Sea Island Carriage Co. features 50- to 55-minute tours using friendly horses that live on a private farm about 10 miles from downtown, where they graze under the shade of live oaks before being transported to town for the tours. Southurn Rose Buggy Tours also features well-cared-for horses (with creative names) on narrated 50-minute tours. Reservations for downtown carriage tours are highly recommended, though not required.

Sea Island Carriage Co.
930 Bay St., Beaufort, 843-476-7789
seaislandcarriagecompany.com

Southurn Rose Buggy Tours
1002 Bay St., Beaufort, 843-524-2900
southurnrose.com

APPRECIATE AUTHENTIC LOWCOUNTRY ART AND HISTORY
AT LYBENSONS' GALLERY

Established in 1977, LyBensons' Gallery in the Frogmore community on St. Helena Island is a treasure trove of African, African American, and Gullah art and history. The former mill is filled to the rafters with rare Benin bronzes, Shona verdite sculptures, a massive collection of colorful Gullah and Lowcountry folk art, sweet grass baskets, jewelry, African Juju hats, black and white photography of famous Black politicians and celebrities, masks, and other rare collectibles. In addition to the artwork, LyBensons' Gallery serves as the Gullah-Geechee Cultural Visitors' Center, with exhibits and videos on the Lowcountry's Gullah community; an exhibit on the life of slave to Civil War hero and US Congressman Robert Smalls; and a selection of history books about the area. It's the perfect spot to begin an exploration of Lowcountry Gullah culture and then take home an authentic souvenir as a reminder of the sacrifice and tenacity of the people who shaped the history of the Southeast.

870 Sea Island Pkwy., St. Helena Island, 843-838-2404
facebook.com/lybensons

76

GLIMPSE INTO THE PAST
IN COLLETON COUNTY

When the British captured Charleston during the American Revolution, the capital of South Carolina was moved to Jacksonboro, part of Colleton County, where the primary cash crops of the area were rice and indigo cultivated on large plantations by enslaved people. The town of Walterborough (now Walterboro) was founded in 1783 and became the county seat in 1817. The Colleton County Historical and Preservation Society was created to protect, preserve, and nurture the cultural heritage of this historical area, with three historic sites under its wing: the 1820 Bedon-Lucas House, one of few remaining "high houses" built to avoid the damp ground of the Lowcountry and help catch summer breezes; the Little Library, Walterboro's oldest public building originally built for the Walterborough Library Society; and Pon Pon Chapel of Ease, the ruins of the 1854 brick building that replaced the original 1735 church.

Bedon-Lucas House
205 Church St., Walterboro

The Little Library
803 Wichman St., Walterboro

Pon Pon Chapel of Ease
Parkers Ferry Rd., Round O

843-549-9633
cchaps.com

77

RELIVE LOCAL HISTORY
AT THE BEAUFORT HISTORY MUSEUM

With colorful and informative photographs, documents, and artifacts, the Beaufort History Museum invites visitors to explore more than 500 years of some of the richest history to be found anywhere in the nation. The museum professionally manages and displays the City of Beaufort's large collection, using it to tell the story of the area's history. Highlights of the permanent collection include the arrival of Indigenous peoples; the first settlers; the European explorations of the early- and mid-16th century; the Revolutionary War; the rice, indigo, and cotton plantation culture; the antebellum decades; secession and the Civil War; Reconstruction; the Spanish-American War; and area growth to present times. There are also pertinent temporary exhibits and many popular events. The museum is located on the second floor of The Arsenal, which was built in 1798 and features fascinating history that can be learned at the museum.

713 Craven St., Beaufort, 843-525-8500
beauforthistorymuseum.org

TIP

The Beaufort area's helpful Visitor Center is also on the ground floor of The Arsenal.

HOP A BOAT
TO QUIET DAUFUSKIE ISLAND

Sandwiched between Hilton Head Island and Savannah and memorialized in Pat Conroy's bestselling book *The Water Is Wide*, Daufuskie Island makes for a unique one- or multi-day trip. It is reached only by boat (including regular ferry service), is just five miles long and less than 2.5 miles wide, and is typically traversed by golf cart. It features a laid-back vibe, quiet coastal landscapes, Gullah history, shopping (like creative coastal metal sculptures from The Iron Fish), varied restaurants, and more. The Daufuskie Difference (daufuskiedifference.com) is a good place to plan a trip, including ferry service; golf cart rentals; tours; Bloody Point Lighthouse; Silver Dew Winery; dining (don't miss the Old Daufuskie Crab Company); and cottage rentals. To see the island like a local, sixth-generation resident Sallie Ann Robinson offers her popular Gullah Tours (gullahtours.org) to island visitors. A renowned chef and cookbook author, Robinson was a student of Conroy when he taught on the island—and she includes her schoolhouse and classroom on her story-filled tours.

hiltonheadisland.org/daufuskie

KID AROUND
AT THE SANDBOX CHILDREN'S MUSEUM

The Sandbox Children's Museum is billed as "an interactive children's museum," but that's just a hint at its playful offerings for families. Located adjacent to Lowcountry Celebration Park, the Sandbox has been successfully disguising learning as play since 2005. Fun interactive exhibits support and encourage development of children through play and learning, including cognitive, emotional and social, health and physical, language and communication, and mathematical thinking and expression. Program offerings are for children ages 1 through 12 and are held weekly, monthly, and throughout the year, including Toddler Time; STEAM Time; Discover, Imagine, Grow (DIG); and varied camps. Finally, the Sandbox offers monthly and annual events for children and their adults, designed around fun themes and holidays, including popular Free Family Fun Night and Imagination Hour.

80 Nassau St., Hilton Head Island, 843-842-7645
thesandbox.org

TIP

Though all are welcome to stop by anytime they're open, reservations for the Sandbox are highly recommended.

EXPLORE LOCAL HISTORY
AT THE EDISTO ISLAND MUSEUM

Operated by the Edisto Island Historic Preservation Society, The Edisto Island Museum opened in 1991 and has continued to expand the collections (and great gift shop) while also working to preserve the island's rich history outside the museum proper. The museum presents extensive and professional historic exhibits, ever-changing art exhibits, and ongoing events. There's also one of two remaining slave cabins from the island (the other one is at the Smithsonian Museum of African American History and Culture). The popular gift shop features arts, crafts, high-quality jewelry, and more from local and regional artists, along with a wide range of Lowcountry-leaning books, toys, and other island-inspired items. The website includes an extensive collection of oral histories that will enhance any visit to the museum and the Edisto area in general. Each October, the "Edisto & Beyond Tour" is a coveted ticket to visit plantations and other historic properties.

8123 Chisolm Plantation Rd., Edisto Island, 843-869-1954
edistomuseum.org

TIP

Be sure to ask about nearby Hutchinson House, thought to be the oldest remaining African American residence in the area. It was built in 1885 by Henry Hutchinson, who was born into slavery at the outset of the Civil War.

Sweetgrass baskets in the Lowcountry
Courtesy of Lowcountry Tourism Commission

SHOPPING AND FASHION

81

BOOK IT
TO A LOWCOUNTRY BOOKSTORE

It's hard to believe that there are so many successful bookstores in the Lowcountry. But, when your literature calling card is Beaufort's beloved Pat Conroy, it's easy to understand why. Conroy's books, legendary book signings, and more created a literary culture that is likely unmatched in any area with the size and population of the Lowcountry (and that's not even counting the multitude of successful bookstores in the Charleston and Savannah areas). Each bookstore has its own atmosphere and specialties. And, following in Conroy's generous wake, there are now dozens of successful authors based in the Lowcountry, and they're often found at bookstores chatting with readers. There is also a plethora of events, book signings, literary gifts, and books for book lovers at the Pat Conroy Literary Center, as well as other well-read Lowcountry literary destinations.

LOWCOUNTRY BOOKSTORES

Beaufort Bookstore

2127 Boundary St., Beaufort, 843-525-1066
thebeaufortbookstore.com

Books-A-Million

11 Robert Smalls Pkwy., Beaufort, 854-240-0707
booksamillion.com

Nevermore Books

910 Port Republic St., Beaufort, 843-812-9460
nevermorebooks.com

McIntosh Book Shoppe

917 Bay St., Beaufort, 843-524-1119

Pat Conroy Literary Center

601 Bladen St., Beaufort, 843-379-7025
patconroyliterarycenter.org

Sassafras on Carteret

206 Carteret St., Beaufort, 843-379-8228
sassafraspost.com

The Storybook Shoppe

1414 Fording Island Rd., Tanger 2-A190, Bluffton, 843-929-1002
thestorybookshoppe.com

Barnes & Noble

20 Hatton Pl., Ste. 200, Hilton Head Island, 843-342-6690
stores.barnesandnoble.com/store/2914

Edisto Island Bookstore

547 Hwy. 174, Edisto Island, 843-869-1885
edistobookstore.com

82

GET YOUR ART ON

AT THE SOUTH CAROLINA ARTISANS CENTER

Featuring the artwork of more than 200 two-stage juried South Carolina master artisans from across 35 of the state's 46 counties, South Carolina's official folk art and craft center in Walterboro features artwork in every medium, including clay, metal, glass, wood, fiber, paper, and mixed media. Highlights include handmade Indigenous folk art using centuries-old craft techniques, contemporary crafts, and two-dimensional art. The curated retail shop showcases Gullah sweetgrass baskets and face jugs, pottery, blown glass, paintings, jewelry, quilts, vases, home furnishings, and agricultural art in every price point throughout the lovingly restored late-1800s eight-room Victorian cottage. The center also offers interpretive displays of Southern folk-life, craft demonstrations, art classes, and other educational events throughout the year that help to preserve and nourish the traditional arts of the region and highlight the handcrafted artwork of the state's leading artists.

318 Wichman St., Walterboro, 843-549-0011
scartisanscenter.com

FEED YOUR KITCHEN HUNGER
AT COOK ON BAY

Located on Bay Street in the heart of Beaufort's charming downtown, this all-things kitchen and cooking boutique is overflowing with coastal cooking tools and serveware. Don't miss their impressive selection of Toadfish shrimp deveiners, crab claw cutters, and oyster knives; locally sourced Lowcountry foods and seasonings, including a great selection of salt grinders and pepper mills; lots of varied cookbooks; kitchen gadgets and implements for every kitchen task; cookware, bakeware, and serveware, including an extensive selection of Le Creuset enameled cast iron; kitchen towels and linens; bar and beverage tools; retro small appliances like kettles, hand mixers, and coffee makers; grilling tools; and a special kids section (for budding young chefs), along with a top-of-the-line knife selection and professional sharpening service. Owned by Jodi Campbell since 2017, the friendly staff are passionate about cooking and baking and love to share their knowledge.

720 Bay St., Beaufort, 843-379-2202
cookonbay.com

FIND THE PERFECT PIECE
IN A LOWCOUNTRY ANTIQUES STORE

With so much history in the Lowcountry, it's no surprise there is a plethora of antiques stores. Historic downtown Walterboro is home to Downtown Envy, an antique mall of more than 50 vendors across three storefronts. Beaufort is home to Bay Street Treasures, located on the ground level basement of the 1840 George Parsons Elliott House, which carries vintage and nearly new furniture and home decor; Collectors Antique Mall, a multi-dealer mall carrying antiques, collectibles, and military memorabilia; and Where'd You Get That, an upscale collection of furniture, home decor, and women's clothing. Unique shops in nearby Yemassee include Barracks Antique Mall, a former barracks used to house Marine recruits coming to boot camp at Parris Island that now stocks a great selection of antiques, collectibles, and vintage, along with a clock shop in the back, and Lowcountry Living Room, a 4,000-square-foot antiques boutique, coffee shop, and event venue.

LOWCOUNTRY ANTIQUES

Downtown Envy

220 E Washington St., Walterboro, 843-549-7219

Bay Street Treasures

1001 Bay St., Beaufort, 843-379-4488
facebook.com/baysttreasures

Collectors Antique Mall

102 Sea Island Pkwy., Beaufort, 843-524-2769
thecollectorsantiquemall.com

Where'd You Get That

9 Marshellen Dr., Beaufort, 843-379-4900
wheredyougetthat.org

Barracks Antique Mall

32 Salkehatchie Rd., Yemassee, 843-441-7442
barracksantiques.com

Lowcountry Living Room

216 US 17 Alternate, Yemassee, 843-384-9650
lowcountrylivingroom.com

85

CHANNEL YOUR INNER ARTIST

AT SOBA GALLERY

Bluffton is a haven for artists and art galleries, with more than a dozen sprinkled throughout Old Town. Founded in 1994 by a group of local artists who had a vision to create a vibrant community arts scene and stimulate future artists, SOBA (Society of Bluffton Artists) Gallery at the corner of Church and Calhoun Streets features original artwork by local and regional artists in a variety of mediums like oil paintings, acrylics, watercolors, handcrafted jewelry, photography, ceramics, sculptures, mixed media, and more. The society also hosts meet-the-artist events, monthly exhibits by member artists, featured artist receptions, and an annual Judged Show that is open to all artists. The SOBA Art School next door hosts workshops and art classes for adults and children from beginners to intermediates, along with summer camps for kids. A piece of artwork from SOBA Gallery makes for the perfect Lowcountry souvenir.

6 Church St., Bluffton, 843-757-6586
sobagallery.com

GATHER, SHOP, AND BE YOU
AT BIRDIE JAMES

With two locations in the Lowcountry, it's easy to be authentically chic at Birdie James. Styling and curating collections for three generations of women is what owner and curator Michelle Taylor and her team do, but the true gem is found in the Birdie James experience. The open-door policy to "gather, shop, and be you" fuels the positive energy of the open floor plan, allowing for endless curation and fashion discovery. With sophisticated collections of textures, prints, and colors in brands such as StitchDrop, Zaket & Plover, Ripley Rader, FARM Rio, and SANCIA, and jewelry brands including Julio Designs, Julie Vos, and Selina King, this is the go-to shop for all the women in your life. They even offer Birdie at Home, a one-time, monthly, or quarterly curated collection of styles handpicked and delivered to your home for you to try on and keep only what you love.

28 Shelter Cove Ln., Ste. 111, Hilton Head Island, 843-842-2622
25 Minetta Ln., Ste. 104, Bluffton, 843-757-2626
thebirdiejames.com

BRING A TOUCH OF SOUTHEAST ASIA INTO YOUR HOME

Although you might not think of Southeast Asian decor in the Southeast United States, Oyster Cay Collection in Beaufort's Old Bay Marketplace imports stunning one-of-a-kind Indonesian and Balinese furniture, accessories, decorative objects, and gift items to add a unique touch to a home or office. The store carries teak chairs, benches, bar stools, cabinets, dining tables, and side tables; woven and natural placemats; hotplates and coasters; decor elements like baskets, trays, plant stands, and decorative statues; and metal, glass, and wood art. They also carry elegant beaded and woven purses, batik scarves, and lounge pants that make the perfect gift (for you or that special someone). In addition to the ever-changing merchandise in the store, they will also help to create the perfect piece for any home using reclaimed teak from their Indonesian furniture artisans. A visit to Oyster Cay Collection will certainly result in one of the more unique souvenirs of a visit to the Southeast.

917 Bay St., Beaufort, 843-525-0485
oystercaycollection.com

88

DO A LITTLE RETAIL THERAPY
AT EGGS'N'TRICITIES

Simply known as "Eggs" to those in the know, Eggs'n'tricities in Old Town Bluffton has been dressing the women (and homes) of the Lowcountry for decades. Located in a historic home that was once in the Pinckney family—as in those South Carolina Pinckneys—the chic boutique is a funky collection of women's clothing, with trendy fashions for the young chicks and more sophisticated looks for the mature hens from brands like Liverpool and Joseph Ribkoff. They also carry handbags of all shapes and sizes and jewelry from hip, costume baubles to unique statement pieces. The back room is a real treasure trove of funky junk, including wall art, vintage decor, barware, seasonal tchotchkes, kitchenware, tableware, and more. The register area is another bounty of gems, from cosmetic bags to eyeglass holders, journals, and other trinkets that make for the perfect gift or that little indulgence that you didn't know you needed.

5 Lawton St., Bluffton, 843-757-3446
eggsntricities.com

89

TAKE HOME A TASTE
OF THE LOWCOUNTRY

With two unique locations in downtown Beaufort and on St. Helena Island, Lowcountry Cider & Superior Coffee provides a duet of shops to get the local lowdown on everything Lowcountry. Plus, they feature many tasty ciders (hot, cold, and to take home), specialty coffee served in a variety of ways, and delectable baked goods, breakfast and lunch sandwiches, and more to enjoy there or later. In addition, there's a large selection of branded jarred offerings (jams, pickled vegetables, salad dressings, and more) and unique home goods and gifts, like beachy kitchen items, books from local authors, and tea towels featuring the paintings of local artists.

102 West St. Ext., Beaufort, 843-524-2326
507 Sea Island Pkwy., St. Helena Island, 843-838-1231
lowcountryciderco.com

TIP

Located on US 17 north of Beaufort, on Charleston Highway running from Charleston to Savannah, always-bustling Carolina Cider Company also features creative ciders of all sorts (peach is particularly popular), baked goods and pies, lots of branded jarred sundries, typical "country store" goods, and Clockwise Coffee.

81 Charleston Hwy., Yemassee, 843-846-1899
carolinaciderco.com

REFLECT ON ART
AT BEAUFORT RIVER GLASS

Originally opened to showcase the beauty and reflection of decorative glass art, Beaufort River Glass has blossomed into a magical gallery of home and garden artwork in Beaufort's downtown shopping district. The colorful and shimmering store showcases stunning works of glistening glass art, including vases, bowls and serving pieces, ornaments, drinkware, paperweights, night-lights, suncatchers, wind chimes, candleholders, garden objects, and other beautiful baubles. There is also a charming selection of creative recycled plastic wall flowers, garden decor, and wall decor from floor to ceiling, as well as ceramic pieces, all kinds of delicate jewelry, glass and mixed-media artwork, and soaps and creams. More than half of the 50 artists represented throughout the store are local, and with much of the artwork paying homage to the natural and coastal environments of the region, the shop makes the perfect art gallery and gift store for the Lowcountry.

812 Bay St., Beaufort, 843-379-5445
beaufortriverglass.com

91

BECOME ONE WITH THE BAREFOOT CONTESSA
AT CASSANDRA'S KITCHEN

Cassandra Schultz grew up in East Hampton, New York, and started working at Ina Garten's specialty food store, the Barefoot Contessa, as a kid, filling bags with Garten's homemade cookies and serving freshly brewed coffee to the customers. Her mother also served as Garten's long-time kitchen assistant. So it's no surprise that Schultz grew up loving the world of cooking and baking. Having been inspired by her cooking idol, she opened a cooking and kitchen emporium with the idea of selling fan-favorite Barefoot Contessa products all in one space. Today, the store carries lots of Garten's favorite brands, products, and even signed cookbooks, along with stunning silver, elegant serving pieces, kitchen tools, pantry items, tabletop and barware, home decor, gift items, and much more. They even offer a bridal registry and gift guide for that extra personal service.

14 Promenade St., Ste. 304, Bluffton, 843-707-1901
cassandraskitchen.com

92

CARRY THE ISLAND SPIRIT WITH SPARTINA 449

Founded by a resident of Daufuskie Island, Spartina 449 started as a marriage of leather and linen—along with whimsical and colorful patterns—to create a timeless women's handbag line that honors the Lowcountry's history. The linen fabric is made from flax harvested in Belgium fields, and the designs are inspired by the island's character and beauty. Company founder Kay Stanley has since morphed her iconic handbags into an upscale women's lifestyle brand featuring apparel, handbags and accessories, belts and scarves, beachwear, jewelry, and more. Named for the lush, green cordgrass that grows in the saltwater marshes of the South Carolina coast and the lot number of her cozy cottage on Daufuskie, Spartina 449 products can be found online, in retailers across the country, their own retail store in Hilton Head, their flagship Bluffton location, and two outlets at Tanger 1 and Tanger 2 in Bluffton.

32 Calhoun St., Bluffton, 843-815-9000
Tanger 1 Hilton Head, 1252 Fording Island, Rd., Bluffton, 843-705-7039
Tanger 2 Hilton Head, 1414 Fording Island Rd., Bluffton, 843-815-2379
28 Shelter Cove Ln., Hilton Head Island, 843-342-7722
spartina449.com

93

SHOP WITH SASS
AT SASSAFRAS ON CARTERET

Beaufort's sprawling shop, Sassafras on Carteret, is a caringly curated gift shop, bookstore, puzzle palace, foodie pantry, children's boutique, and much more. Their large book collection ranges from local books and authors to bestsellers, new releases, classics, varied bibles, and local history books, as well as literary-leaning merchandise (think bookmarks, book tote bags, writing utensils, mugs, shirts, tea towels, and loads of clever cocktail napkins). Their puzzle collection is wide-ranging, with hundreds of possibilities for adults and kids. The laundry list of gift-giving possibilities also includes clothing, jewelry, handbags, spa and bath, gardening, and cooking and cuisine (including lots of tasty options produced in the Lowcountry). Sassafras on Carteret owner Susanne Scott Blumer has three other popular shops in North Carolina, including Sassafras on Main and Minted Mercantile in Waynesville, and Sassafras on Sutton in Black Mountain. For sassy shoppers from near and far, Sassafras on Carteret is a must-see and -shop Lowcountry destination.

206 Carteret St., Beaufort, 843-379-8228
sassafraspost.com

BASK IN BIVALVE BRIC-A-BRAC AT BLUFFTON GENERAL STORE

It's hard not to get caught up in the oyster culture in the Lowcountry. Especially since the estuaries, riverbanks, salt marshes, creeks, and tidal areas that surround the region are the perfect home for oyster beds. Fortunately, you can find tons of anything-but-ordinary oyster paraphernalia to bedeck your home (or for the perfect Lowcountry souvenir) in Old Town's Bluffton General Store. From notecards and ornaments to painted serving trays, tea towels, plates, napkins, books, spoon rests, jewelry, decorative art, and more—many created by local artists—bivalve art rules. But if oysters aren't your thing, never fear. This boutique general store is filled with all kinds of other coastal-inspired artwork, maps, kitchen and barware, pillows, soaps, candles, foodstuffs, books about the area, T-shirts, socks, mugs and glassware, a kids' section, games, puzzles, and so many more things you didn't know you needed.

12 Church St., Bluffton, 843-837-4675
blufftongeneralstore.com

FILL YOUR GLASS
AT TA·CA·RÓN

Halfway between Beaufort and Bluffton lies an unsuspecting wine shop that is both mellow and complex, just like good wines should be. Owned by Cuban-born Juan Carlos Jiménez and his wife, Isabella, ta·ca·rón features an impressive selection of obscure boutique wines you won't find in grocery or big box stores. Stocking unique wines mostly from South America, Europe, New Zealand, Australia, South Africa, and the United States (although you won't find many California wines), ta·ca·rón also sells its own private label fresh-roasted coffee, plus its own portfolio of Cuban seed cigars manufactured in the Dominican Republic. With a focus on traditional wine regions like France, Italy, Spain, Chile, and Argentina, as well as up-and-coming regions like Uruguay, Portugal, South Africa, and Slovenia, ta·ca·rón prides itself on introducing its customers to new grape varieties. The intimate store also hosts monthly wine tastings, private tastings, themed wine events, and the highly successful ¡SALUD! Wine Club.

6983 N Okatie Hwy. 170, Ridgeland, 843-812-9938
tacaron.com

TIP

The owners advertise Cuban hours, otherwise known as Friday and Saturday (and most Thursday afternoons), "noonish" to 4 p.m. But if you spot the red convertible out front with license plate "CIGARRR," you are welcome to stop in.

96

CELEBRATE AMERICAN CRAFTS
AT WITH THESE HANDS GALLERY

Located on Edisto Island, With These Hands Gallery has been paying homage to handmade American crafts since 1984. Representing local and nationally recognized artists, the shop carries an extensive collection of handmade paintings, pottery, glass, wood, textiles, and jewelry. The works are curated by owner Carolyn Kelsey Wilson through her travels, art shows, and word of mouth. Many pieces focus on the beauty of the Lowcountry, with stunning beach and marsh scenes; local wildlife photography; and decorative art pieces using shells, driftwood, sea glass, and other beach finds. In addition to wall decor and decorative art pieces, they also carry vases, floral arrangements, candles, outdoor art, kitchen and tabletop pieces, apparel, handbags, bath and body, kids' clothing and toys, and games and puzzles. They even sponsor an annual giving tree fundraiser during the holidays, with artists painting one-of-a-kind ornaments. Whether decorating a home or giving gifts, beautiful and creative pieces await in-store or online.

547 Hwy. 174, Edisto Island, 843-869-3509
withthesehandsgallery.com

97

GET EVERYTHING FOR THE HOME
AT GRAYCO HARDWARE & HOME

Founded in Beaufort in 1961 and still going strong for locals and visitors alike, beloved Grayco Hardware & Home has practically anything and everything for homes, gift giving, and more. The company's continued success is still based on the principles of professional and friendly customer service and giving back to the Lowcountry communities where they're based. Grayco is a Lowcountry go-to one-stop destination for hardware, plumbing and electrical, paint supplies, seasonal and outdoor living (including a sprawling and varied grilling section), lawn and garden, Lowcountry-leaning home decor, home goods, furniture, upholstery, clothing, and so much more, with locations in Beaufort and Hilton Head. They also have separate building and remodeling locations in Beaufort, Bluffton, and Ridgeland. If you can't find it at Grayco Hardware & Home, you probably don't need it.

6 Bow Cir., Hilton Head Island, 843-785-5166
136 Sea Island Pkwy., Beaufort, 843-521-8060
graycoinc.com

MAKE YOUR WAY
TO MACDONALD MARKETPLACE

Macdonald MarketPlace on St. Helena Island was built as a community corner store by James Ross Macdonald in 1877 and was a long-time hub of social and business activity. Though it had many lives over the years, generations later, the Macdonald family is once again running the store James founded. Thanks to the Sanders family (of nearby Seaside Farm and Seaside Grown fame), Macdonald MarketPlace has a mission of uniting local artisans in one collective space. Different areas have different "themes," but the shop generally focuses on local art, antiques, and the home. A lot of their offerings are coastal leaning in some way, whether one is furnishing a Lowcountry home or taking back a bit of the coast. A large corner room at the front of Macdonald MarketPlace features foodstuffs and more for the gourmand, including a great wine selection and many popular options from Seaside Grown, like their famous Bloody Mary mixes.

853 Sea Island Pkwy., St. Helena Island, 843-838-1810
macdonaldmarketplace.com

99

ROLL ON OVER
TO ROLLERS WINE & SPIRITS

Rollers Wine & Spirits on Hilton Head Island is like a candy store for adults when it comes to shopping for wine, spirits, non-alcoholic beverages, mixers, cigars, gourmet foodstuffs, and more. Featuring a sprawling main store on Palmetto Bay Road, as well as two convenient smaller outposts, Rollers Wine & Spirits offers one-stop shopping for a variety of imbibing, and they pride themselves on providing friendly and knowledgeable staff, including certified sommeliers who can help select the perfect wine for any meal or occasion. Rollers also features a wine bar, very popular wine tastings and other events, more than a dozen different cigar brands, and a large selection of domestic and imported cheeses and cured meats, as well as gift baskets. Even for those not staying on Hilton Head Island, Rollers Wine & Spirits is a worthwhile destination. However, be sure not to drink and drive; roll with a designated driver.

9 Palmetto Bay Rd., Hilton Head Island, 843-842-1200
6 Lagoon Rd., Hilton Head Island, 843-785-3614
95 Mathews Dr., Hilton Head Island, 843-681-8454
rollerswineandspirits.com

100

GO BIG
ON THE PIG

Gene Martin's Red & White opened in Coligny Plaza in 1969 as Hilton Head Island's first grocery store, and today, as Piggly Wiggly Coligny Plaza, it remains an island institution. Gene Martin's son, David, has run the beloved island Pig for decades, and he's carried on his father's legacy of friendly and personalized service. Of course, today's modern Piggly Wiggly features competitively priced groceries, but there's much more to this iconic store. The seafood is mostly local and fresh, and the tasty shrimp is steamed for free upon request. The friendly meat market will prepare special cuts, and the bustling deli features Boar's Head meats. They also offer a wide range of local and regional foodstuffs, like varied jams and jellies, Seaside Grown Bloody Mary mixes and more, and Marsh Hen Mill grits and other offerings. Beach needs are easily met, and they also carry a huge selection of popular Pig memorabilia, including T-shirts, keychains, magnets, Tervis tumblers, koozies, and coffee cups.

1 N Forest Beach Dr., Hilton Head Island, 843-785-3881
pigglywigglyhiltonhead.com

ACTIVITIES
BY SEASON

SPRING

Get Your Groove On with Street Music on Paris Avenue, 51
Praise the Past at Old Sheldon Church Ruins, 98
Watch Golf Greats at the RBC Heritage Golf Tournament, 63
Get Carried Away by a Carriage Tour in Historic Beaufort, 103
Eat Farm-to-Fork at FARM, 26
Get Outside with Coastal Expeditions, 62

SUMMER

Get on the Water with Edisto Watersports & Tackle, 74
Splash into the Beaufort Water Festival, 44
Beach It on Hilton Head Island, 82
Listen to Live Music on the Water at Pressley's at the Marina, 53
Support Local Farmers at Lowcountry Farmers Markets, 22
Get on Two Wheels with Wheelz Hilton Head, 65

FALL

Say Cheers to Shellring Aleworks, 24

Stay in a CCC-Built Cabin on the Edisto River, 73

Quench Your Thirst at Burnt Church Distillery, 6

Nurture Nature at Pinckney Island National Wildlife Refuge, 66

Learn to Cook at the Culinary Institute of the South, 18

Get Out on the Spanish Moss Trail, 77

WINTER

Enjoy Dinner and a Movie at Park Plaza Cinema, 50

Enjoy Daily Live Music Year-Round at Tiki Hut, 40

Get Healthier at Hilton Head Health Wellness Resort & Spa, 72

Make Music at the Kazoobie Kazoo Museum & Factory, 56

Roll on Over to Rollers Wine & Spirits, 132

Rub Elbows with the Stars at the Beaufort International Film Festival, 54

SUGGESTED ITINERARIES

TASTES OF THE LOWCOUNTRY

Eat Everything but the Oink at Rizer's Pork & Produce, 10
Take Home a Taste of the Lowcountry, 122
Learn to Cook at the Culinary Institute of the South, 18
Dive Deeply into Southern Cooking at Bucky's Seafood, 14
Taste the Lowcountry at Lowcountry Produce, 2
Support Local Farmers at Lowcountry Farmers Markets, 22

SAY CHEERS

Say Cheers to Shellring Aleworks, 24
Roll on Over to Rollers Wine & Spirits, 132
Drink and Eat Well at Blacksheep X Sabbatical, 33
Enjoy Daily Live Music Year-Round at Tiki Hut, 40
Fill Your Glass at ta·ca·rón, 128
Quench Your Thirst at Burnt Church Distillery, 6
Get Your Fill of Live Music, Grub, and Views at The Fillin' Station, 57

COUPLES

Get Healthier at Hilton Head Health Wellness Resort & Spa, 72
Dine in a Mansion at Ribaut Social Club, 9

Praise the Past at Old Sheldon Church Ruins, 98
Enjoy Dinner and a Movie at Park Plaza Cinema, 50
Bring a Touch of Southeast Asia into Your Home, 120
Explore a Lowcountry Paradise at Montage Palmetto Bluff, 68

FAMILY AFFAIRS

Beach It on Hilton Head Island, 82
Slither Over to Edisto Island Serpentarium, 71
See the Making of Marines at Parris Island, 99
Go Wild in Walterboro, 70
Kid Around at the Sandbox Children's Museum, 108
Get Carried Away by a Carriage Tour in Historic Beaufort, 103

HISTORY LESSONS

Explore Local History at The Edisto Island Museum, 109
Glimpse into the Past in Colleton County, 105
Honor America's History at the Reconstruction Era National Historical Park, 94
Learn about the Lowcountry's Rich Gullah Culture, 100
Celebrate Gullah Culture at Historic Penn Center, 90
Relive Local History at the Beaufort History Museum, 106
Explore America's First Self-Governed Town of Freedmen, 102

GET OUTSIDE

Get on Two Wheels with Wheelz Hilton Head, 65
Get Out on the Spanish Moss Trail, 77

Enjoy Disc Golf and the Water at Sergeant Jasper Park, 67
Experience Primitive Lowcountry Coastline Life at Botany Bay, 80
Nurture Nature at Pinckney Island National Wildlife Refuge, 66
Spend the Day at the Beach at Hunting Island State Park, 60

WATER LOVERS

Get Outside with Coastal Expeditions, 62
Bask in Bivalve Bric-a-Brac at Bluffton General Store, 127
Get on the Water with Edisto Watersports & Tackle, 74
Taste the Sea at Locals Raw Bar, 13
Hop a Boat to Quiet Daufuskie Island, 107
Plunge into Lowcountry Marine Heritage, 89
Get Adventurous with Outside Hilton Head, 69

TAKE IN THE ARTS

See a Show at the Arts Center of Coastal Carolina, 46
Rub Elbows with the Stars at the Beaufort International Film Festival, 54
Channel Your Inner Artist at SOBA Gallery, 118
Listen Up at the Jazz Corner, 45
Get to Know the Prince of Scribes at the Pat Conroy Literary Center, 88
Support All the Arts at the Center for the Arts, 42
Get Your Art On at the South Carolina Artisans Center, 114

INDEX

41 UP, 20
ACE Basin, 62, 64, 70, 74, 93
ACE Basin Fish Camp, 25
Alder Lane Beach, 83
Alexander Bache US Coast Survey Line, 80
Anchorage 1770, 9
Arcuri, Tony, 12
Arsenal, The, 106
Art Market at Historic Honey Horn, The, 92
Arts Center of Coastal Carolina, 46
Atlantic Dunes by Davis Love III, 78
Backus Bakery, 100
Bank, The, 6
Barefoot Contessa, 124
Barefoot Farms, 23
Barnes & Noble, 113
Barracks Antique Mall, 116–117
Bay Street Treasures, 116–117
Beach House Hilton Head Island, 40–41
Beaufort, 2, 5, 7, 9, 13, 17, 28–29, 30, 33, 36–37, 42, 44, 48–49, 51, 54, 56, 57, 60, 62, 77, 86–87, 88, 89, 90, 94–95, 99, 101, 103, 106, 112–113, 115, 116–117, 120, 122, 126, 128, 130
Beaufort Bookstore, 113
Beaufort County, 44, 77
Beaufort History Museum, 106
Beaufort International Film Festival, 42, 54–55
Beaufort River Glass, 123
Beaufort Tours, 48
Beaufort Visitor Center, 86–87, 106
Beaufort Water Festival, 44
Bedon-Lucas House, 105
Beedos Burgers, 61
Benny Hudson Seafood, 20
Benny's Coastal Kitchen, 20
Big Chill, The, 48, 54, 103
Birdie James, 119
Bistro, The, 18–19
Black Mountain, 126
Blacksheep X Sabbatical, 33
Bleak Hall Plantation, 80
Bloody Point Lighthouse, 107
Bluff Plantation, 49
Bluffton, 6, 18, 21, 22, 26, 28–29, 31, 34–35, 36–37, 66, 68, 86–87, 100, 113, 118, 119, 121, 124, 125, 127, 128, 130
Bluffton BBQ, 37
Bluffton General Store, 127
Bluffton Gullah Cultural Heritage Center, 6, 100
Bluffton Pasta Shoppe, 35
Blumer, Susanne Scott, 126
Boar's Head, 133
Books Sandwiched In, 42
Books-A-Million, 113
Botany Bay Heritage Preserve and Wildlife Management Area, 80
Brick Baptist Church, 90, 94
Bruff, Rebecca, 95
Bubba Gump's House, 49
Bucky's Seafood, 14
Bull, William, 98
Bullies BBQ, 37
Burkes Beach, 82–83
Burnt Church Distillery, 6
Cahill's Market & Chicken Kitchen, 28–29
Camp Saxton, 94

Campbell, Jodi, 115
Carb, Steve, 12
Carolina Cider Company, 122
Carolina Heritage Outfitters, 73
Carson, J. J., 34
Carter, Brandon, 26
Cassandra's Kitchen, 124
Center for the Arts at the University of South Carolina Beaufort, 42, 55
CharBar Co., 12
Charleston, xv, 30, 70, 105, 112, 122
Choo Choo BBQ, 37
Citadel, The, 88
Civilian Conservation Corps (CCC), 64, 73
Clist Café, 18–19
Clockwise Coffee, 122
Coast at Sea Pines Beach Club, 79
Coastal Discovery Museum, 22, 92
Coastal Expeditions, 62
Coastal Restaurants and Bars (CRAB), 20–21
Coligny Beach, 40, 82
Coligny Beach Park, 65, 82–83
Collectors Antique Mall, 116–117
Colleton Civic Center and Hampton St. Auditorium, 47
Colleton County, 47, 93, 105
Colleton County Historical and Preservation Society, 105
Colleton Museum & Farmers Market, 23, 93
Colleton State Park, 73
Common Thread, 26
Conroy, Pat, v, 48, 75, 88, 91, 107, 112
Cook on Bay, 115
Cottage Cafe, Bakery & Tea Room, The, 34
Cozart, Hunter and Jessie, 13
Crescendo, 52
Culinary Institute of the South, 18
Darrah Hall, 94
Daufuskie Difference, The, 107
Daufuskie Island, xv, 7, 69, 86, 88, 107, 125
Daufuskie Island Distillery, 7
Dempsey Farms, 23
Donnelley Wildlife Management Area, 76
Downtown Catering, 31
Downtown Deli, 31
Downtown Envy, 116–117
Driessen Beach Park, 83
Duffy, Krista, 33
Dukes Barbecue, 36
Duke's BBQ, 36
Duvall, Robert, 48
Dye, Pete, 78
Edisto Beach, 32, 53, 64
Edisto Beach State Park, 64, 73
Edisto Bike Rentals, 74
Edisto Island, xv, 8, 23, 53, 64, 71, 74, 80, 109, 113, 129
Edisto Island Bookstore, 113
Edisto Island Historic Preservation Society, 109
Edisto Island Museum, The, 109
Edisto Island Serpentarium, 71
Edisto River Adventures, 73
Edisto River Canoe & Kayak Trail, 73
Edisto Watersports & Tackle, 74
Eggs'n'tricities, 121
Estill, 36
FARM, 26
FARM Hospitality Group, 26
Farmers & Makers Market, 22
Farmers Market of Bluffton, 22
Farmers Market of Hilton Head, 22, 92
Feret, Phillippe, 4
Fiddler's Seafood, 97

Fillin' Station Waterfront Bar & Grill, The, 57
Fish and Grits Music Festival, 52
Fish Haul Beach Park, 83
Fishcamp on 11th Street, 25
Fishcamp on Broad Creek, 25
Flora and Fauna, 26
Flow Gallery + Workshop, 68
Folly Field Beach Park, 83
Foodseum, 18
Forrest Fire BBQ, 37
Forrest Gump, 47, 48–49, 54
Four Square Gospel Church in *Forrest Gump*, see Stony Creek Presbyterian Chapel
Frampton Plantation House and Lowcountry Visitors Center, 86–87
Fraser, Charles, 63
Fraser's Tavern, 79
Fripp Island, 75, 86
Fripp Island Golf & Beach Resort, 75
Frogmore, 104
Gantt, Hastings, 90
Gantt Cottage, 90
Garten, Ina, 124
Gay Fish Company, 49
George & Pink's, 23
George Shearing Quintet, 45
Giuseppi's Pizza & Pasta House, 12
Givhans Ferry State Park, 73
Grayco Hardware & Home, 130
Great Santini, The, 48, 88, 103
Green Pond, 76
Greenbow Elementary in *Forrest Gump*, see Colleton Civic Center
Gullah Grub, 91
Gullah Tours, 107
Gullah-Geechee Cultural Visitors' Center, 104
Gump House, The in *Forrest Gump*, see Bluff Plantation
Hale Tea Co., 30
Hampton, 28–29, 43
Hampton County, 43
Hampton St. Auditorium, 47
Harbour Town, 78
Harbour Town Bakery & Café, 79
Harbour Town Golf Links, 63, 79
Harbour Town Lighthouse, 78
Hardeeville, 28, 67
Hardeeville Chiken Lickn, 28
Harold's Country Club, 16
Harvey, Kathy Conroy, 88
Hearth Wood Fired Pizza, 17
Herban Market & Cafe, 5
Heron Point by Pete Dye, 78
Hilton Head Distillery, 7
Hilton Head Health Wellness Resort & Spa, 72
Hilton Head Island, ii, 2, 4, 6–7, 8, 12, 20–21, 22, 25, 27, 36–37, 40–41, 45, 50, 52, 58, 63, 65, 67, 69, 72, 78, 82, 83, 86, 87, 89, 92, 102, 107, 108, 113, 125, 130, 132, 133
Hilton Head Island-Bluffton Chamber of Commerce and Visitor & Convention Bureau, 87
Hilton Head Island Recreation, 52, 67
Hilton Head Island Jam, 52
Hilton Head Wingfest, 52
Hilton Head Social Bakery, 4
Historic Mitchelville Freedom Park, 83, 102
Hover Links at First Presbyterian Church, 67
Hudson's Seafood House on the Docks, 27
Hunting Island, 49, 60–61, 62, 86
Hunting Island State Park, xiv, 49, 60
Hurt, William, 48
Hutchinson, Henry, 109

Hutchinson House, 109
Indigo Spa, 72
Inn & Club at Harbour Town, 78
Iron Fish, The, 107
Islanders Beach Park, 82–83
Jackson, Stonewall, 34
Jacksonboro, 25, 105
Jasper County, 67
Jazz Corner, The, 45
Jeep Island, 52
Jiménez, Juan Carlos and Isabella, 128
John Mark Verdier House, 101
Johnson Creek Tavern, 61
Juice Hive, The, 35
Kazoobie Kazoo Museum & Factory, 56
King, Martin Luther, Jr., 90
King Bean Coffee, 30
King's Farm Market, 23
Kline, Kevin, 48
Lady's Island, 13, 29, 86
Latinos Unidos Food Festival, 52
Le Creuset, 115
Legends Golf Course, 99
Lesesne, Amy, 9
Lester's Country BBQ, 36
Links, 79
Listen on the Lawn, 42
Little Library, The, 105
Lobeco, 2
Locals Raw Bar, 13
Lodge, 10
Loniero, Jim, 12
Love, Davis, III, 78
Lowcountry Celebration Park, 52, 108
Lowcountry Cider & Superior Coffee, 122
Lowcountry Living Room, 116–117
Lowcountry Produce, 2, 79
Lucky Duck Distillery, 7
Lunch with the Authors, 42
LyBensons' Gallery, 104
Ma Daisy's Porch, 6, 100
Macdonald, James Ross, 131
Macdonald MarketPlace, 131
Magnolia Cafe, 30–31
Marina at Edisto Beach, 53
Marine Corps Recruit Depot Parris Island, 99
Marsh Hen Mill, 34, 133
Martin, David, 133
Martin, Gene, 133
Martin Family Park, 22
Maryland Fried Chicken, 28–29
Masteller, Bob and Lois, 45
Masteller, David, 45
Masters, The, 63
May River Coffee Roasters, 35
McIntosh Book Shoppe, 113
Meccariello, Rick, 12
Meggett, 8
Miller High Life, 33
Mitchel, Ormsby, 102
Minted Mercantile, 126
Montage Palmetto Bluff, 68
Moon King Entertainment Group, 6
Morris, Danny, 96
Morris Center for Lowcountry Heritage, 96
Naval Heritage Park, 22
Nectar, 12
Nevermore Books, 113
Nicklaus, Jack, 63
Oglethorpe, James Edward, 98
Okatie, 89
Old Bay Marketplace, 120
Old Daufuskie Crab Company, The, 107
Old Town Bluffton, 26, 34, 121
Old Sheldon Church Ruins, 98

One Hot Mama's, 37
Outside Hilton Head, 69
Oyster Cay Collection, 120
Palmer, Arnold, 63
Palmetto Bluff Farm, 68
Palmetto Theater, 43
Park Plaza Cinema, 50
Parris Island, 48, 99, 116
Party in the Park + Maker's Fair, 52
Pat Conroy Literary Center, 88, 112–113
Pat Conroy Literary Festival, 42, 88
Penn Center, 90–91, 94
PGA TOUR, 63
Piggly Wiggly Coligny Plaza, 133
Pinckney, Charles Cotesworth, 66
Pinckney Island National Wildlife Refuge, 66
Pistol Jo's Cherry Point BBQ, 36
Plums, 17
Poseidon, 12
Pon Pon Chapel of Ease, 105
Port Royal, 21, 22, 24, 25, 27, 36–37, 51, 77, 82, 86, 94, 99
Port Royal Cypress Wetlands and Rookery, 51
Port Royal Farmers Market, 22
Port Royal Sound Foundation Maritime Center, 89
Pressley's at the Marina, 53
Price, Lantz, 17
Prince of Tides, The, 48, 54, 88
Q on Bay, 37
Q's Chicken Shack, 28–29
Quarterdeck, 79
Quarterdeck Market, 79
RBC Heritage, 63
Radio, 47
Rails to Trails Conservancy, 77
Rec Graveyard, 67
Reconstruction Era National Historical Park, 94
Ribaut Social Club, 9
Ridgeland, 7, 23, 36, 96, 128, 130
Rigdon's Fried Chicken, 28–29
Rizer's Pork & Produce, 10–11
Roadhouse, 37
Robinson, Sallie Ann, 107
Rohland, Leslie, 34–35
Rollers Wine & Spirits, 132
Rotten Little Bastard Distillery, 7
Round O, 105
Roxbury Mercantile, 8
St. George, 73
St. Helena Island, 23, 49, 61, 62, 86, 90–91, 104, 122, 131
St. Helena Memorial Gardens, 91
St. Helena Parish Chapel of Ease, 91
St. Phillips Island, 60, 62
Saltus River Grill, 17
Salty Dog Cafe, The, 79
Salty Dog Cruise, 89
Sandbox Children's Museum, The, 108
Sarge Disc Golf Course, The, 67
Sassafras on Carteret, 113, 126
Sassafras on Main, 126
Sassafras on Sutton, 126
Savannah, xv, 26, 30, 70, 98, 107, 112, 122
Schultz, Cassandra, 124
Sea Pines Resort, The, 63, 78
Seaside Farm, 131
Seaside Grown, 131, 133
SERG (Southeast Entertainment Restaurant Group), 12
SERG Takeout Kitchen, 12
Sea Island Carriage Co., 103
Sea Pines Beach Club, 79
Sea Turtle Patrol Turtle Talks, 52

Sergeant Jasper Park, 67
Shell Ring Oyster Company, 27
Shellring Aleworks, 24
Sherman, William Tecumseh, 98
Shinetown Moonshine, 7
Shops at Sea Pines Center, The, 22, 78
Shrimp Shack, 61
Side Hustle Brewing Company, 6
Silver Dew Winery, 107
Skull Creek Boathouse, 12
Smalls, Robert, 95, 104
Smithsonian Museum of African American History and Culture, 109
Smokehouse at Paris Avenue, The, 37
SOBA Gallery, 118
South Beach, 82–83
South Carolina Artisans Center, 114
South Carolina Barbecue Trail, 36
South Carolina Chef Ambassador, 26, 34
South Carolina Department of Natural Resources, 76
Southurn Rose Buggy Tours, 103
Spanish Moss Trail, 77
Spartina 449, 125
Squire Pope Carriage House, 86–87
Stanley, Kay, 125
Stony Creek Presbyterian Chapel, 49
Story Fest, 96
Storybook Shoppe, The, 113
Strange Bird, 26
Street Music on Paris Avenue, 51
Superior Coffee, 122
Surfside Market, 79
Symphony Under the Stars, 52
ta·ca·rón, 128
Taylor, Michelle 119
Technical College of the Lowcountry (TCL), 18
Tervis, 133
Tiki Hut, 38, 40–41
Toadfish, 115
Town of Ridgeland Farmers Market, 23
Town's Holiday Kick-off Festival, 46
Trouble the Water, 95
True restaurant, 72
Tucker, Ron and Rebecca, 54
Turner, Ted, 60
Turtle Talks, 52
UDisc, 67
US Fish and Wildlife Service, 66
USCB Center for the Arts, 55
Varn's General Store, 93
Verdier, John Mark, 101
Voices of Gullah, 46
Wallace, Matt, 33
Walterboro, 14, 23, 36, 47, 49, 70, 73, 93, 105, 114, 116–117
Walterboro Wildlife Center, 70
Walterboro Wildlife Sanctuary, 70
Waynesville, 126
Whaley's Restaurant & Bar, 32
Water Is Wide, The, 107
WHAM! Festival (Walterboro History, Art, and Music Festival), 47
Wheelz Hilton Head, 65
Where'd You Get That, 116–117
Wildflower Cafe on Telfair Square, 26
Williams, Wille J. "Bucky," 14
Williams Seafood, 14–15
Wilson, Carolyn Kelsey, 129
WiseGuys, 12
With These Hands Gallery, 129
Yemassee, 7, 16, 49, 87, 98, 116–117, 122
Young, Dillard and Lindsey, 74